The First-Year English Teacher's Guidebook

The First-Year English Teacher's Guidebook offers practical advice and recommendations to help new English teachers thrive in the classroom. Each chapter introduces a concept crucial to a successful first year of teaching English and discusses how to incorporate that concept into your daily classroom practice. You'll find out how to:

- Clearly communicate instructional goals with students, parents, and colleagues;
- Incorporate students' out-of-school interests into the curriculum;
- Use assignment-specific rubrics to respond to student writing in meaningful ways;
- Integrate technology into ELA instruction;
- Conduct student-centered writing conferences;
- Make time for self-care and self-improvement;
- and much, much more.

Additionally, the guidebook provides a number of forms, templates, graphic organizers, and writing prompts that will enable you to put the author's advice into immediate action. These tools are available for download on the book's product page: www.routledge.com/9781138495708.

Sean Ruday is an Associate Professor of English Education at Longwood University and a former classroom teacher. He is also a Co-President of the Assembly for the Teaching of English Grammar. He frequently writes and presents on innovative ways to improve students' literacy learning.

The First-Year English Teacher's Guidebook

Strategies for Success

Sean Ruday

Routledge
Taylor & Francis Group

NEW YORK AND LONDON

First published 2018
by Routledge
711 Third Avenue, New York, NY 10017

and by Routledge
2 Park Square, Milton Park, Abingdon, Oxon, OX14 4RN

Routledge is an imprint of the Taylor & Francis Group, an informa business

© 2018 Taylor & Francis

Library of Congress Cataloging-in-Publication Data
A catalog record for this book has been requested

ISBN: 978-1-138-49569-2 (hbk)
ISBN: 978-1-138-49570-8 (pbk)
ISBN: 978-1-351-02370-2 (ebk)

Typeset in Palatino and Formata
by Apex CoVantage, LLC

Download the eResources at www.routledge.com/9781138495708

Contents

Meet the Author vii
Acknowledgments ix
eResources xi

Introduction: What Do New English Teachers Need? 1

Section 1: Instructional Strategies 5
  1 Clearly Communicate Instructional Goals 7

  2 Incorporate Students' Out-of-School Lives. 17

  3 Understand the Connection Between Instructional Procedures
     and Student Behavior 27

  4 Integrate Technology Purposefully 39

Section 2: Assessment Strategies 49
  5 Use Assignment-Specific Rubrics. 51

  6 Respond to Student Writing in Meaningful and Useful Ways 65

  7 Conduct Student-Centered Writing Conferences. 75

  8 Utilize Exit Questions 85

Section 3: Work-Life Balance Strategies 95
  9 Communicate Actively and Carefully with Students
     and Families 97

  10 Work Effectively with Mentors. 107

  11 Make Time for Self-Care 117

Section 4: Resources 125
  12 Key Takeaway Ideas 127

References 131
Appendix A: Forms, Templates, and Graphic Organizers 133
Appendix B: A Guide for Book Studies. 149
Appendix C: Recommendations for Mastering ELA Content Knowledge 151

Meet the Author

Sean Ruday is an Associate Professor of English Education at Longwood University. He began his teaching career at a public school in Brooklyn, NY, and has taught English and language arts in New York, Massachusetts, and Virginia. Sean is a Co-President of the Assembly for the Teaching of English Grammar—a grammar-focused affiliate of the National Council of Teachers of English. He is the founder and editor of the *Journal of Literacy Innovation* and the editor of the *Virginia English Journal*. Some publications in which his articles have appeared are *Journal of Teaching Writing*, *Journal of Language and Literacy Education*, *Contemporary Issues in Technology and Teacher Education*, and the *Yearbook of the Literacy Research Association*. His professional website is seanruday.weebly.com. You can follow him on Twitter @SeanRuday. This is his eighth book with Routledge Eye on Education.

Acknowledgments

I am filled with gratitude for the fantastic individuals who helped make this book possible:

- The wonderful teachers who shared their thoughts and gave me the opportunity to work with them and their students.
- The amazing students whose ideas, insights, and writings are included in this book.
- This book's editor, Lauren Davis, whose guidance and support has been integral to the creation of this book and to my work as a writer.
- Brittany Pierce Herndon, who shared with me important insights about the experiences of new English teachers.
- My parents, Bob and Joyce Ruday, for encouraging me to pursue my dream of becoming a teacher.
- My wife, Clare Ruday, who brightens my life by bringing humor and happiness to it.

eResources

The appendices of this book can also be downloaded and printed for classroom use. You can access these downloads by visiting the book product page on our website: www.routledge.com/9781138495708. Then click on the tab that says "eResources," and select the files. They will begin downloading to your computer.

Introduction
What Do New English Teachers Need?

I've done a lot of professional development sessions in my career, focusing on pretty much every aspect of grammar and writing instruction, but I recently conducted one that was unlike the others. I was asked to talk to the new middle and high school English teachers in a school district, with the objective of giving them strategies and ideas to help them be as successful as possible in their first years of teaching. A couple of months prior to this, I spoke with an administrator for this school district, who explained that the district wanted me to share some advice with the new English teachers: "We have a lot of new English teachers, and we want to give them more support," she shared with me. "We want them to be successful and to stay teaching with us; we really don't want to lose them."

This administrator's concerns were certainly well-founded: research shows that 40% to 50% of new teachers leave the profession in their first five years (Ingersoll, 2003), and that schools that serve high-need populations (as many in this school district and around the country do) experience the highest level of new-teacher turnover (Sutcher, Darling-Hammond, & Carver-Thomas, 2016). In addition, middle and high school English teachers bring home copious amounts of papers to grade, which provides another potential cause of burnout (Jago, 2005). In a conversation with the previously mentioned administrator about providing professional development for new English teachers, she explained, "We give new teachers a bunch of information about the details of the schools where they're working, but we don't really talk with them about how to be a new teacher. We need to give our new teachers more support like that."

"Plus," she continued, "giving our new teachers more support is important to our students' learning. Students who learn from a thriving teacher will learn a lot more than those who learn from a struggling one."

All of these insights show how it essential it is that new teachers are well-supported, which is where I came in: to provide new middle and high school English with strategies for navigating the challenges they'll face in their new careers. When the professional development session for these teachers began, I felt a rush of excitement: "I'm thrilled to be talking with you all today. You're at such an important time—in your professional lives and in your lives in general. Today, we're going to begin a conversation about strategies for making your first year as an English teacher as successful as possible, which will also help you be a happy and productive English teacher for the rest of your career."

During the rest of that session, and in several subsequent meetings, I talked with these teachers about many practical and research-based ideas for succeeding as new English teachers; the information we discussed formed the foundational ideas for this book. As this vignette suggests, the issue of supporting new English teachers is important to the successes of those individuals, to their students, and to the teaching profession in general. In this introductory chapter, I provide an overview of some of the ideas that are essential to this text: 1) why I decided to write this book, 2) what to expect in this book, and 3) how to maximize the benefits of this book.

Why I Decided to Write This Book

When I was first contacted to talk with new middle and high school English teachers about ways to make their first years as successful as possible, I did a lot of reflecting on my first year in the classroom as a full-time teacher. During that first year—in which I taught seventh-grade English at a public middle school in Brooklyn, NY—I experienced many challenges, but also some significant successes. I was challenged by the difficulties of classroom management and the paper grading workload, but also had great success making connections to my students' out-of-school lives and helping them develop as writers. For example, I conducted student-centered activities such as using hip-hop lyrics to teach reading and writing strategies and used assessment practices such as writing conferences and assignment-specific rubrics to help the students enhance their writing skills.

Thinking back on my experiences as a new teacher led me to also consider what resources are available for new English teachers. I examined the professional literature, finding a number of books that give advice to new teachers and many books that provide practical suggestions for English teachers, but nothing that merged both topics to provide classroom-ready recommendations specifically for new English teachers. I believe that there are issues and challenges specific to the work of new English teachers that can't be covered in books written for new teachers of all subjects, nor can they be properly addressed in books written for all English teachers. For example, research indicates that new teachers are primarily challenged by classroom management, lack of guidance and resources for unit and lesson planning, and insufficient levels of support (Goodwin, 2012), but no professional book that I've seen has dealt with those issues and others like them with the specific experiences of new English teachers in mind.

What to Expect in This Book

I've designed this book to provide information specifically for new English teachers, focusing on recommendations that are geared toward the experiences of those who are teaching that subject for the first time. The strategies in the text are divided into three key sections: Section One focuses on instructional strategies, Section Two describes assessment strategies, and Section Three addresses work-life balance strategies. There are four instructional strategies addressed in Section One: clearly communicate instructional goals, incorporate students' out-of-school lives, understand the connection between procedures and student behavior, and integrate technologically purposefully. Section Two discusses four assessment strategies: use assignment-specific rubrics, respond to student writing in meaningful and useful ways, conduct student-centered writing conferences, and utilize exit questions. The work-life balance strategies described in Section Three help new English teachers avoid burnout while doing their jobs well: communicate actively and carefully with students and families, seek mentorship networks, and make time for self-care.

All of these recommendations are practitioner-oriented, designed to help new English teachers understand key ideas that will maximize their successes. Each chapter in these three sections is divided into four components: a "What Is It?" section, which provides an overview of the concept discussed in the chapter; a "Why Does It Matter?" section, which discusses why the concept is important to a successful first year of teaching English; a "What Does It Look Like in Action?" section, which describes how I've put the chapter's topic into action in my work as an educator and consultant; and a "Key Tips" section, which conveys key suggestions for new English teachers as they incorporate the chapter's ideas into their own work. (Note that each "What Does It Look Like in Action?" section that describes a teaching practice discusses how I put that idea into action with a ninth-grade English class. I chose ninth grade for this purpose because it's in the middle of the grade levels that this book addresses, resulting in it having components that can be connected to all of the grades discussed in the text.)

This book also contains a fourth section, which focuses on practical resources for teachers to use: Chapter Twelve provides a conclusion that discusses final takeaway ideas for putting the insights in this guidebook into action; Appendix A contains reproducible forms, templates, and graphic organizers that teachers can photocopy and integrate into their instruction; Appendix B is a guide for book studies, a list of thought-provoking questions, prompts, and connections that groups who are using this text as a book study can use to guide their conversations and analyses; and Appendix C contains specific suggestions for mastering ELA content knowledge, such as texts, writing strategies, and grammatical concepts I recommend teaching in grades six through twelve. The recommendations in Appendix C are based on the Common Core State Standards as well as my own research, classroom experiences, and conversations with students and teachers. Section Four also includes a list of references that can be used by those interested in conducting further reading about sources that have informed the ideas presented in this book.

How to Maximize the Benefits of This Book

If you're a new English teacher reading this book to help you succeed during your first year of teaching, or if you're studying to become an English teacher and want to learn how to succeed in your future career, congratulations! You're doing the kind of professional development reading that will help you accomplish great things as a teacher—not just this year, but in every year of your career. I recommend maximizing the benefits of this book by thinking of the information in each of the book's sections as separate components of being a strong teacher. Imagine that you're an athlete trying to make every part of your skill set as strong as possible; just as a good baseball player needs to be able to throw, run, and hit, you'll want to ensure that your instructional, assessment, and work-life balance skills are all on point. I've worked with new English teachers who are amazing instructors, but struggle with assessment-related strategies, such as providing students with assignment-specific feedback that relates to their current zones of proximal development. I've also met teachers who have good understandings of instructional and assessment strategies, but really struggle with using the work-life balance strategies essential to avoiding burnout.

Mastering these three skill sets will allow you to have a productive, successful, and enjoyable first year as an English teacher and will give you important strategies that you can continue to apply throughout your career. The first year of teaching is exciting and inspiring, but can also be very challenging. Fortunately, you have this resource to guide you through the process and maximize your chances for having a successful year. If you're ready to begin the journey of your first year as an English teacher with me as your guide, keep reading!

Section 1

Instructional Strategies

1

Clearly Communicate Instructional Goals

In this first chapter, we'll examine an important aspect of effective instruction: clearly communicating the instructional goals of a class period. We'll begin by looking at what this instructional strategy is and then consider why it's important to the work of a new English teacher. Next, we'll take a look at a description of how I put this idea into action with a ninth-grade English class. Finally, we'll consider some key recommendations to help you clearly communicate instructional goals to your students.

What Is It?

The teaching technique of clearly communicating the instructional goals for a specific class meeting is more complex than one might initially think. When talking with the new English teachers mentioned in the introductory chapter, I explained that it's one thing to simply write instructional goals on the whiteboard (many state departments of education require that teachers display the state standards or Common Core Standards being covered in that day's lesson), but another to communicate that information clearly and meaningfully. "People will tell you to write on the board the name and number of the state standard you're addressing that day, and that's a requirement, so you should definitely do it," I told the new teachers. "However, what's going to really resonate with your students isn't whether or not the state standard being addressed is written in the classroom, but rather how clearly and effectively you've communicated specific instructional goals for that day's lesson."

I continued to explain that state and Common Core Standards are usually general, but specific instructional objectives that an effective teacher establishes for a lesson are much more concrete and direct. For example, Common Core Writing Standard W.9–10.2 calls for students to "Introduce a topic; organize complex ideas, concepts, and information to make important connections and distinctions; include formatting (e.g., headings), graphics (e.g., figures, tables), and multimedia when useful to aiding comprehension" (Core Standards, 2010). That's a lot of information! In fact, since there's so much information in this standard, writing it on the board won't give the students clear understandings of what they'll be studying that day.

One of the ways I recommend clearly communicating a day's instructional goals is through the use of big questions, which are questions that address the essential learning outcomes and main ideas you'll address in the day's lesson. For example, when recently talking with ninth-grade students about the impact of relative clauses on effective writing, I displayed the big questions illustrated in Figure 1.1.

These questions clearly convey to students the two major learning objectives for the day; after examining these questions, students will know what we'll be talking about the features of relative clauses and discussing why they're important.

The second strategy I recommend using to clearly communicate a lesson's goals is displaying the day's agenda. Figure 1.2 conveys the agenda I used in the lesson that addressed the previously mentioned big questions about relative clauses.

Showing an example such as this one clearly communicates the learning activities for the day, setting the tone for the lesson by sharing with the students what the class is expected to accomplish. This example shows how the class will begin (with a fast write, which is a form of low-stakes writing) and end (with an exit question). In addition, it communicates how the teacher will describe the day's topic and previews how the students will apply their understandings of it. Now that we've considered two ways to clearly introduce instructional goals at the beginning of a class, let's think together about why these tactics are important to effective instruction.

Figure 1.1 Examples of Big Questions

Big Questions

◆ What are the characteristics of relative clauses?

◆ Why are relative clauses important tools for effective writing?

Figure 1.2 Example of an Agenda

Agenda

- ◆ Fast write
- ◆ Mini-lesson: Attributes of relative clauses
- ◆ Discussion: Examples from literature
- ◆ Group work: Analysis activity
- ◆ Exit question

Why Does It Matter?

When recently speaking with new English teachers about clearly communicating the instructional goals for a class period, I was quick to emphasize the importance of this strategy: "It's important for all teachers to get their students engaged and ready to work at the very beginning of class, but it's especially important when you're a new teacher and you're still getting comfortable with classroom management and the challenge of getting students focused and ready to learn. Students come into our classrooms from the hallways, where their minds are occupied with issues like 'Should I go to the party this weekend?' 'Will we win the game tonight?' and 'Is that cute brunette going out with anyone?' With these important middle and high school–related issues on their minds," I said smiling, "it's essential that we take steps to help our students focus at the beginning of class. By introducing big questions and agendas to our students, we help make this happen." In this section, we'll look specifically at big questions and agendas and consider why each of these tactics is important to effective instruction.

Big Questions

The effective use of one or more big questions at the beginning of a lesson is comparable to a strong lead in of a piece of writing; both of these tactics grab the attention of the audience and introduce key information that will be addressed in more detail in the near future. To illustrate this, let's compare the big questions depicted in Figure 1.1 with the opening lines of this book: the big questions "What are the characteristics of relative clauses?" and "Why are relative clauses important tools for effective writing?" get the students' attention while also introducing important information. Similarly, this book's first two sentences read:

> I've done a lot of professional development sessions in my career, focusing on pretty much every aspect of grammar and writing instruction, but I recently conducted one that was unlike the others. I was asked to talk to the new middle and high school English teachers in a school district, with the objective of giving them strategies and ideas to help them be successful as possible in their first years of teaching.

These sentences are designed to communicate the main focus of the book in a way that interests readers and encourages them to keep reading. As you create big questions for your classes, think of them as leads for your lesson that grab your students' attention and focus them on the key topics you'll address.

Agendas

Agendas are important to effective instruction because they list the activities that will help the class answer the big questions, which helps set a serious and scholarly tone for the events of the class period. When I go over the day's agenda with my students, I like to call attention to the amount of work on it and use this statement to emphasize how hard we'll work that day. After I introduced the agenda depicted in Figure 1.2 to my students, I explained, "There's a lot for us to do today, but I know we can do it. We'll work hard, but we'll also learn a lot and be able to answer the big questions for the day's lesson." Several new English teachers I've worked with have told me that they struggle with getting students focused at the beginning of class without threatening discipline; I've found describing the day's agenda is a great way to deal with this problem because it communicates to students in a professional and respectful way, "We need to work hard today."

Figure 1.3 summarizes why big questions and agendas are effective ways to clearly communicate a day's instructional goals.

Figure 1.3 Why Big Questions and Agendas Are Important

Instructional Strategy	Why the Strategy Is Important
Big Questions	Big questions grab students' attentions introduce key information that will be addressed in more detail in the lesson.
Agendas	Agendas list the activities that will help the class answer the big questions, which helps set a serious and scholarly tone for the events of the class period.

In our next section, we'll take a look inside a classroom and check out a snapshot description of me using big questions and agenda items to clearly communicate instructional goals to my students.

What Does It Look Like in Action?

"Did you see what she posted on Instagram?!"

"Yes! I can't believe it!"

It's a Friday morning and my ninth graders' thoughts are consumed by their friends' Instagram posts, LeBron James' basketball statistics, their weekend plans, and many other topics not directly related to school. However, in English class today, we'll be talking about the writing strategy of acknowledging alternate and opposing claims in argument essays. I'm going to introduce our big questions and agenda items to the class to help them focus on the day's topics.

"Good morning, everyone," I greet the students. "It's great to see you! Let's get started by taking a look at today's big questions."

I display the slide depicted in Figure 1.4 that introduces our focal questions for the day and read the questions out loud.

"During our work today," I explain, "we're going to discuss the answers to these big questions. Once our class is done, you'll be able to answer these three questions about acknowledging alternate and opposing claims in argument essays."

"Now that we've checked out the big questions," I continue, "let's take a look at our agenda for today's class, which tells us what activities we'll do today that will help us answer the big questions." The slide featured in Figure 1.5 illustrates the agenda I shared with the students.

"As you can see," I tell the students, "there's a lot on our agenda, which means we'll need to work hard and be efficient with our class time.

Figure 1.4 Big Questions about Acknowledging Alternate and Opposing Claims

Big Questions

◆ How do writers acknowledge alternate and opposing claims in their argument essays?

◆ Why is this an important aspect of strong argument essays?

◆ How can we apply this strategy to our own essays?

Figure 1.5 Agenda for Acknowledging Alternate and Opposing Claims

Agenda

- ◆ Anticipation guide
- ◆ Mini-lesson: What are does it mean to acknowledge alternate and opposing claims? Why is this a good idea?
- ◆ Examples of strong acknowledgments of alternate and opposing claims
- ◆ Group discussion: Identify and analyze acknowledgments of alternate and opposing claims
- ◆ Individual work: Acknowledge alternate and opposing claims in your own essays
- ◆ Exit question

Even though the agenda is full, I know we can accomplish everything on it. Once we complete these activities, you'll have excellent understandings of the strategies of acknowledging alternate and opposing claims. Now, let's get started!"

Key Tips

In this section, we'll examine two suggestions that can make your implementation of the instructional strategies discussed in this chapter as effective as possible: 1) increase complexity in big questions and 2) gradually release responsibility in agenda items. Each of these suggestions can ensure that your students feel both challenged and supported throughout the course of a lesson. Now, let's consider each of these suggestions in detail by exploring what each one means and exactly why it can be beneficial.

1   Increase complexity in big questions.

When creating the big questions that will inform the day's instructional goals and activities, I recommend starting with fundamental questions about the basic features of concepts and moving to more advanced stages of understanding and application. For example, the two big questions on relative clauses described earlier in this chapter begin with a question about the fundamental attributes of the concept ("What are the characteristics of relative clauses?") and then move to a more cognitively advanced question that asks students to consider the impact of the concept ("Why are relative clauses important tools for effective writing?"). Similarly, the big questions on acknowledging alternate and opposing claims in argument writing discussed in the chapter's teaching example start by addressing basic understandings of the strategy, then move to analyzing the strategy's importance, and finally focus on students applying the strategy to their own works.

I recommend constructing big questions for your students by working backwards, thinking first about what ultimate goal you have for your students and then thinking about what understandings they'll need to reach those goals. Then, you can create one or two big questions that address the fundamental components of a concept and one or two questions that deal with its significance and application—I recommend creating no more than two or three big questions for each lesson. For example, if your goal is for students to apply sensory details to their writings, you might start with a big question about what sensory details are, then follow that with one that asks why they are important to effective writing, and conclude with a question that addresses how students can use sensory details to improve their own works. This sequence of questions will communicate to students the information they'll be learning in that day's class and how their work with that information will increase in complexity.

The planning template depicted in Figure 1.6 will help you construct big questions to use with your students. (A reproducible version of this form is available in Appendix A.) This template identifies the two instructional focuses that big questions should address (the fundamental components of a concept or topic and its significance or application), provides a space for you to write your own questions related to a topic, and lists examples of questions discussed in this chapter.

Figure 1.6 Big Question Planning Template

Instructional Focus	Question(s) Related to Instructional Focus	Examples
Fundamental components		How do writers acknowledge alternate and opposing claims in their argument essays?
Significance and application		Why is this an important aspect of strong argument essays?
		How can we apply this strategy to our own essays?

2. Gradually release responsibility in agenda items.

This recommendation is conceptually related to the previous one: just as I suggest organizing the big questions based on increasing complexity, I recommend constructing the agenda items based on the idea of gradual release of responsibility, an instructional strategy that calls for students to take increased ownership of their learning as they continue to work on a concept (Fisher & Frey, 2003). Both of these suggestions are based on the idea that students should gradually move from basic understandings to higher-order thinking skills such as analysis and application. A lesson that gradually releases responsibility employs a "to, with, and by" approach (Campbell, 2009) in which the teacher explains a strategy to students (the "to" portion), engages them in a collaborative discussion or activity that incorporates the strategy (the "with" component), and then asks students to put their understanding of it into practice (the "by" section).

The two agenda examples featured in this chapter represent the gradual release of responsibility approach; the agenda for the lesson on acknowl-edging alternate and opposing claims in argument writing moves from a mini-lesson on the topic to a group discussion in which students identify examples of these concepts and then to an individual activity in which students apply the day's focal strategy to their own works. The activities in the relative clause agenda are slightly different, as this lesson moves from a mini-lesson on the attributes of relative clauses to a discussion of examples of these concepts in literature and then to group analysis activ-ity, but the lesson still gradually releases responsibility to students. While there are different ways the "to, with, and by" components can be put into action, it's important to include all three aspects into an instructional agenda: doing so can help you create a learning environment for your stu-dents that's both supportive and challenging.

Figure 1.7 provides a template to use when constructing an agenda to use with your students that focuses on planning the "to, with, and by" com-ponents of the lesson. It contains places to write each of these instructional

Figure 1.7 "To, With, and By" Agenda Planning Template

Agenda Section	Activity	Example Activity
To		Mini-lesson on activity acknowledging alternate opposing claims.
With		Group discussion of identifying and analyzing acknowledgments of alternate and opposing claims.
By		Students work on acknowledging alternate and opposing claims in their own works.

aspects as well examples of from the agenda I used when teaching ninth graders about acknowledging alternate and opposing claims. (A reproducible version of Figure 1.7 is available in Appendix A.)

Final Thoughts on Clearly Communicating Instructional Goals

- ◆ I believe it's important for new teachers to understand the difference between writing instructional goals on the whiteboard (in the form of a state or Common Core Standard) and communicating that information clearly and meaningfully.
- ◆ Two tactics I recommend using to clearly and meaningfully communicate instructional goals are big questions and agendas.
  - ◆ Big questions are questions that address the essential learning outcomes and main ideas you'll address in the day's lesson.
  - ◆ Agendas communicate the learning activities for the day, setting the tone for the lesson by sharing with the students what the class is expected to accomplish.
- ◆ Big questions are important to effective instruction because they grab students' attentions and introduce key information that will be addressed in more detail in the lesson.
- ◆ Agendas are important because they list the activities that will help the class answer the big questions, which helps set a serious and scholarly tone for the events of the class period.
- ◆ When constructing big questions and agenda items to use with your students, keep these recommendations in mind, as following them will help your students feel both supported and challenged:
  - ◆ Increase complexity in big questions.
  - ◆ Gradually release responsibility in agenda items.

2

Incorporate Students' Out-of-School Lives

This chapter explores an extremely important strategy for new English teachers to master: incorporating students' out-of-school lives into in-class activities and assignments. First, we'll examine what this strategy is and then reflect on its significance to effective instruction. After that, we'll check out an example of how it can look in action with a ninth-grade English class. Then, we'll conclude by considering some important suggestions that can help you maximize the effectiveness of this strategy with your students.

What Is It?

This instructional strategy incorporates students' out-of-school lives in ways that help them learn academic material. The specific ways it takes shape in the classroom depend on the students you're teaching and the instructional focus for a lesson or activity. For example, a lesson on strong leads might ask students to examine the opening lines of popular songs and reflect on how they grab the listener's attention and introduce key content just as a strong lead in a story or essay should do. Similarly, a lesson on prepositional phrases can call for sports-fan students to identify prepositional phrases in sports writing and reflect on how those phrases add important description to a passage. While these examples vary based on the academic focus and particular texts being integrated, they all apply academic thinking and analysis to information that students encounter in their out-of-school lives.

It's essential that English instruction that involves students' out-of-school lives makes clear connections to the academic material students

Figure 2.1 Examples of Out-of-School Texts and Academic Connections

Out-of-School Texts	Academic Connections
Opening lines of popular songs	Strong leads in stories and essays
Descriptive language in sports writing	Prepositional phrases and sensory imagery
Addressing friends on social media	The use of vocatives (nouns of direct address) in speaking and writing
Terminology associated with technological communication	The use of strong verbs and specific nouns for clarity

are learning (Duncan-Andrade & Morrell, 2005; Ladson-Billings, 1995). In other words, it's not enough for a lesson to bring in a high-interest song or popular culture connection; the out-of-school material must be used as a vehicle for learning (Duncan-Andrade & Morrell, 2005; Ladson-Billings, 1995). I recently explained this idea to a group of new English teachers: "When you give students an opportunity to bring in material from their out-of-school lives, make sure you've established a strong connection between that material and what you're teaching them. This creates a concrete academic focus for the lesson, which will help you teach and help your students learn." (This idea is discussed in more detail in the key tips section later in this chapter.)

Figure 2.1 lists some examples of out-of-school texts that can be used to help students learn academic material. Check out these possible connections; after that, we'll consider the importance of this strategy to effective English instruction.

Why Does It Matter?

Facilitating connections between material that is relevant to students' out-of-school lives and academic topics is a key component of effective English instruction for three reasons: it facilitates student engagement, it makes new material less intimidating, and it encourages students to rethink academic concepts. In this section, we'll examine each of these benefits in detail, considering how they build off each other and why each one is related to making connections to students' out-of-school lives.

Facilitating Student Engagement

Think about the last time you took part in some kind of professional development, such as attending a workshop, reading a professional book like this one, or a checking out a blog post that described a teaching activity.

If you're like me, you really appreciated it when the presenter or author worked hard to get you excited about the topic: emphasizing its importance, relating it to other topics that interest you, or beginning in an interesting way. Our students appreciate it when we do this for them as well. When I recently taught ninth graders about the importance of vocatives by making connections to their social media use (I describe this lesson in more detail a bit later on in this chapter), several students told me at the end of class that they found the out-of-school connections engaging in ways that helped them learn the material. One explained, "I love how you related what we were learning about today to things we do when we use Twitter. It made the lesson more interesting and easier to understand." Another commented, "I had a lot of fun in English today because I was interested. Since I was interested and was having fun, I learned more than usual." Since engaging our students through connections to their out-of-school lives helps get them interested in a topic, it represents an important step toward crafting an effective lesson.

Making New Material Less Intimidating

Integrating material that relates to students' out-of-school lives also has the potential to enhance student learning by making new material less intimidating. Some grammatical concepts, reading strategies, and writing tactics can be difficult for students to grasp, but these challenging topics can become more accessible when presented in the context of familiar material relevant to students' out-of-school interests. For example, I recently worked with a high school English class on the grammatical concept of subordinate clauses. Many students in the class were unfamiliar with the attributes of this concept and how it can be used to enhance a piece of writing. After I discussed the fundamental aspects of subordinate clauses, I showed the students some examples of them in popular music and asked them to then work in small groups to identify lyrics of songs they enjoy that contained subordinate clauses. When students shared the examples they identified, I asked them why they felt the subordinate clause they found was important to the song in which it appeared. This activity allowed students to connect high-interest song lyrics with a challenging grammatical concept, creating an environment that the students found comfortable and conducive to an enjoyable learning activity.

Encouraging Students to Rethink Academic Concepts

When students learn how to apply academic strategies to out-of-school texts, they rethink the purpose of the skills, strategies, and concepts they learn in school: instead of thinking of academic skills as only relevant to work they do in the classroom, students begin to see these skills as also having relevance to the ways they understand and interpret material they interact with outside of school. For example, if a student is asked to identify subordinate clauses in popular song lyrics of her or his choice, that student won't just see subordinate clauses as something that has relevance to English class: she or he will see this concept as important to fully understanding all kinds of texts, including popular music. Similarly, if a student who is interested in sports looks for examples of prepositional phrases in sports writing, that individual will have a different perspective on prepositional phrases than one who only works with this concept on worksheets. The student that makes connections to out-of-school texts will understand that writers of all genres can use prepositional phrases to enhance their works; the one that isn't encouraged to make these connections may not make these same connections. Creating opportunities for students to connect skills, strategies, and concepts they learn in school to texts that represent aspects of their out-of-school lives helps them see that these ideas don't just exist in school-based activities: they are useful for understanding all kinds of texts.

These three benefits—facilitating student engagement, making new material less intimidating, and encouraging students to rethink academic concepts—represent important reasons why incorporating aspects of students' out-of-school lives into English instruction can make our students' experiences as effective as possible. Figure 2.2 lists each of these benefits and summarizes the importance of each one.

In the next section, we'll take a look inside a ninth-grade English class and see how I use the students' social media use to help them understand the concept of vocatives.

Figure 2.2 Benefits of Incorporating Students' Out-of-School Lives

Benefits	Explanations
Facilitates student engagement	Students become more interested in the material, which can help lead to them understanding it better.
Makes new material less intimidating	Students can find challenging topics to be more accessible when those topics are presented in the context of familiar material relevant to students' out-of-school interests.
Encourages students to rethink academic concepts	Students can see how the skills, strategies, and concepts they learn in school also have relevance to the ways they understand and interpret material they encounter outside of school.

What Does It Look Like in Action?

"Get ready," I begin today's class period by telling my ninth graders. "Today, we're going to totally rethink the concept of vocatives."

In the previous day's class, I talked with students about vocatives—words and phrases used to direct a statement toward someone or something, such as the word "Kate" in the sentence "Thank you, Kate." We discussed the fundamental features of this concept and looked together at some examples of how it's used. In today's lesson, we're going to have a lot of fun with vocatives while also deepening our understandings of the topic: we'll make connections to how students use vocatives when communicating on social media to directly address someone or something.

"Now that we know what vocatives are," I explain, "we're going to think about a scenario in which you often see them: on social media sites like Twitter, Facebook, and Instagram." The students seem to perk up with this connection and I continue, "There are times on these platforms where you'll direct a statement specifically to another person using her or his screenname. For example, my name on Twitter is @SeanRuday, so you could use a vocative to tweet 'I can't wait for your English class today, @SeanRuday.'" A few students laugh at this example and I elaborate: "However, it's important to note that using someone's screenname doesn't always mean you're using a vocative. For example, if you tweeted, 'I love @SeanRuday's English class,' you wouldn't be you using a vocative because you wouldn't be using my screenname to direct a statement specifically to me."

I display Figure 2.3, which contains these two example tweets and explanations of why each one does or does not contain a vocative, on the document camera.

I review this information with the students, highlighting the idea that words and phrases function as vocatives if they direct a statement

Figure 2.3 Tweets and Vocative Explanations

Example Tweets	Explanations of Vocative Use
I can't wait for your English class today, @SeanRuday	This statement contains a vocative: @SeanRuday is a vocative because it directs the tweet to a particular individual.
I love @SeanRuday's English class	This statement does not contain a vocative: @SeanRuday is used to identify the teacher of the class, but this screenname does not direct the statement to a specific person like in the previous tweet.

to someone or something, but that those same words and phrases can be used in other ways if they are meant as a form of direct address.

After this explanation, I introduce the next activity: "Your job is to work in small groups and find an example of a social media post someone in the group has created that uses a screenname as a vocative, as well as one that uses a screenname in a non-vocative way. The first example tweet I showed you today is an example of one that uses a screenname as a vocative, while the second one is an example of one that uses a screenname in a non-vocative way." I briefly review the content of each example and then continue: "To complete this activity, you'll want to look back through old social media content the people in your group have created for examples that fit these categories. If these categories don't apply to your old posts, work with your group members to find some from their old posts that do. While you complete the activity, I'm going to give you a graphic organizer to fill out that asks you to write down the social media post you selected and an explanation of how it does or does not use a screenname as a vocative." (This graphic organizer is depicted in Figure 2.4; a reproducible version is available in Appendix A.)

I give a graphic organizer to each group and circulate the room as the students begin to work, listening intently while they scroll through their social media profiles discuss whether certain screenname mentions are vocatives. When the groups seem to be close to completing the activity, I begin to sit down with them and ask about their findings. I first meet with a group of students seated near the front of the room that seems especially engaged in the activity: "I love how into this you all were," I open the conversation, smiling. "Talk to me about what you found."

Figure 2.4 Graphic Organizer for Vocative Social Media Analysis

Social Media Post	Explanation of How It Does or Does Not Use a Screenname as a Vocative

"We used two examples from my Twitter," begins a boy in the group. "The first one we found has a vocative. It says, 'happy birthday' and then my friend Cooper's Twitter name."

"Yeah," continues another student in the group, "and it uses the screenname as a vocative because it makes the message in the tweet directed to Cooper. The vocative directs the message of 'happy birthday' to him."

"Very nicely done!" I respond. "You all did a great job of identifying an example of a tweet that uses a screenname as a vocative and explaining why it does so. Now, talk to me about the next example—the one that uses a screenname in a non-vocative way."

"For that one," states the student who originally shared, "we found one of my tweets about one of my basketball teammates. It says, 'I just saw' and then his screenname 'dunk a basketball!'"

"Good job identifying this," I reply. "Now, let's talk about the next topic: why does this tweet use the teammate's screenname in a non-vocative way?"

"Because it uses his screenname, but doesn't direct the statement just to him," he answers.

"It says that I saw him dunk a basketball. If it said, 'Hey,' his screenname, 'I just watched you dunk,' it would be a vocative because it would direct the statement to him, but this tweet doesn't do that."

"Awesome!" I exclaim. "I love how you used an example of how that tweet look if it did include a vocative. You all did a very nice job of identifying these tweets and explaining the role of the screennames in them."

I then proceed to move around the classroom, meeting with the other student groups and finding myself similarly impressed with their identifications and analyses. Before the end of the class period, I ask the students to comment on how this activity went: "What was this activity like for you? What did you think about looking at social media posts and analyzing them for the uses of vocatives?"

"I loved it!" shouts a female student in the front row. "It was fun and it made learning about vocatives really relevant since we could see ways we use vocatives when use social media."

"I think it helped me understand vocatives better," interjects another student, "especially analyzing how screennames can be vocatives sometimes but not others and why. That helped me understand a lot better."

Key Tips

In this section, we'll consider two important recommendations that can help your inclusion of students' out-of-school lives work as well as possible: 1) provide a clear academic focus and 2) let the out-of-school connections come from the students. By following these suggestions, you'll maximize the effectiveness of this strategy by increasing both academic rigor and student engagement, two important aspects of effective instruction. Let's explore each recommendation by examining what each one means and why it can beneficial.

1. Provide a clear academic focus.

Learning activities that facilitate connections to students' out-of-school lives are most effective when we teachers provide the students with clear academic guidelines for integrating out-of-school content. For example, if I want to create an activity in which my students bring in high-interest song lyrics, I'll increase its chance of effectiveness if I first establish an academic focus for it. Earlier in this chapter, I discussed a time when I asked students to apply their understandings of subordinate clauses by identifying examples of them in song lyrics and analyzing why those subordinate clauses are important to the songs in which they appeared. In addition to incorporating high-interest content, this activity also provided students with a clear academic focus for the lesson.

Providing these clear academic guidelines helps us teachers maximize the effectiveness of our lessons by making them both engaging and academically valuable. I think of learning activities that incorporate students' out-of-school lives as balancing acts: the best ones include a number of opportunities for relevant and engaging connections, but do so within the framework of important and challenging academic content. When planning activities and lessons that make connections to students' out-of-school interests, I recommend using the planning guide depicted in Figure 2.5 (and available in reproducible form in Appendix A); the guide asks you to identify the academic topic on which you're focusing, the related out-of-school content, and why you believe the out-of-school content connects to the academic topic.

I like this planning guide for two reasons. First, it helps me be certain that I'm connecting academic material to out-of-school material, ensuring that my lessons containing these connections are both engaging for my students and academically meaningful. Second, completing the planning guide gives me a concrete and pedagogically sound way to justify my choices to incorporate high-interest material into my classes. For example, if an administrator or parent asked me why I was using song lyrics in a lesson on subordinate clauses or social media in an activity about vocatives, my responses on the planning guide would defend my choices and convey my rationales.

2. Let the out-of-school connections come from the students.

Another key to a successful lesson that incorporates out-of-school connections is to allow those connections to come directly from the students. One way to think of this suggestion is that we teachers are the experts of

Figure 2.5 Out-of-School Content Planning Guide

Academic Topic on Which You're Focusing	Related Out-of-School Content	Why You Believe the Topic and Content Relate

academic content, while our students are the experts in what they find relevant and engaging. With this in mind, we can teach our students about academic concepts such as writing strategies, literary themes, and grammatical concepts, and then give our students opportunities to apply that academic information to material they find relevant. The instructional descriptions in this chapter provide examples of this suggestion, such as the activity where I asked students to find subordinate clauses in song lyrics and the one in which I challenged them analyze whether or not screennames on social media were used as vocatives. (Remember to use your judgment about inappropriate lyrics in the classroom—I recommend establishing a clear expectation for students that the song lyrics they incorporate need to be school-appropriate to prevent this from becoming an issue.) In each instance, I provided the students with instruction about the features and attributes of the academic topics and then gave them opportunities to find examples of those topics in material relevant to their out-of-school interests.

Giving students these opportunities to identify relevant examples ensures that they feel ownership of the activity. If we didn't provide these opportunities, students wouldn't have the same chance to bring in material that relates to the lesson's academic focus and to their interests. I recently spoke the ninth-grade students that participated in the vocatives and social media lesson about the importance of the opportunity to bring in their own content: one student explained, "It was really cool that you let us bring in our own examples from our own Twitters and other [social media]. It was a lot more interesting and made it so we could personally relate to what we were doing a lot more." Another student added, "Yeah, we were learning, but it was still about us."

Final Thoughts on Incorporating Students' Out-of-School Lives

◆ This instructional strategy connects content from students' out-of-school lives to academic concepts they learn in English class, such as writing tactics, reading strategies, and grammatical concepts.

◆ Facilitating connections between material that is relevant to students' out-of-school lives and academic topics is a key component of effective English instruction for three reasons: it facilitates student engagement, it makes new material less intimidating, and it encourages students to rethink academic concepts.

   ◆ It facilitates student engagement by helping them become more interested in the material.

   ◆ It makes new material less intimidating because students can find challenging topics to be more accessible when those topics are presented in the context of familiar material relevant to students' out-of-school interests.

   ◆ It encourages students to rethink academic concepts because it helps them see how the skills, strategies, and concepts they learn in school also have relevance to the ways they understand an interpret material they encounter outside of school.

◆ When incorporating material relevant to students' out-of-school lives into your English instruction, I recommend following two key recommendations that can increase both academic rigor and student engagement:

   ◆ Provide a clear academic focus.

   ◆ Let the out-of-school connections come from the students.

3

Understand the Connection Between Instructional Procedures and Student Behavior

In this chapter, we'll work to understand a key component of effective teaching: the connection between instructional procedures and student behavior. First, we'll consider how these concepts are related and then reflect on why this connection is important to the development of new English teachers. After that, we'll examine how I put this strategy into practice with a ninth-grade English class. We'll then conclude by exploring some key suggestions to help you use this idea with your students.

What Is It?

Classroom management skills and instructional abilities are sometimes considered to be two totally separate aspects of a teacher's skill set, like a performer who is being evaluated on his or her acting and dancing abilities. In reality, however, the instructional procedures we teachers implement and the behavior of our students are closely connected: having a clearly organized, well-paced, and thorough lesson plan is essential to strong classroom management. I recently spoke to a group of new English teachers about the relationship between classroom management and instructional procedures, helping them identify connections between the two entities: "When you think about a teacher with strong classroom management abilities, you might think about someone who has been teaching for a long time and has a really tough demeanor. When I first started teaching, that's what I thought was needed for a teacher to be effective at classroom management. Once I was in the classroom for a little while, I realized I didn't need those things—which was good because I hadn't been teaching for long and I'm not a particularly tough-looking person! Instead, I learned that I needed strong and well-structured instructional

Figure 3.1 Lesson Components to Strong Classroom Management

Component	Description
Clear organization	A structured lesson plan for students to follow that includes a posted agenda and a clearly communicated procedure for students to follow at the beginning of class.
Strong sense of pace	A lesson that moves relatively briskly, while still allowing for students to have enough time needed to complete the tasks on which they are working.
Thorough lesson plan	A plan that includes many varied learning activities so that students are engaged in a number of ways there isn't any empty time at the end of a class period or a need to make activities take longer than they should.

procedures and activities; if I had those, I would effectively manage my students' behaviors."

Figure 3.1 describes the three components of an effective lesson I've identified as important to strong classroom management: clear organization, a strong sense of pace, and a thorough lesson plan.

Why Does It Matter?

In this section, we'll take a closer look at the instructional procedures that I've identified as important to classroom management and consider the significance of each one. Each explanation addresses how the instructional aspect is important to student behavior.

Clear Organization

Clearly organized instructional procedures communicate to students that they're in an environment where learning is taken seriously and that they are expected to behave in ways that are conducive to learning. If students walk into a classroom where the learning activities are well structured and clearly communicated, the students will have no trouble figuring out what to do when they're in the classroom. While clearly communicating the day's activities to the students doesn't stop every possible classroom management issue, it does send a message that there are clear and rigorous expectations regarding what will be done in class, which can contribute to a class period running smoothly and effectively, with minimal disruptions. During my first year of teaching, I was pleasantly surprised by the positive impact that having a posted agenda and a well-organized series of related activities had on my students' behaviors: organizing my learning activities and communicating that organization by going over the agenda at the beginning of class and reminding students of it throughout the period went a long way toward maximizing the effectiveness of my classroom management.

One especially effective way to enhance the enhance the organization and structure of a class period is having a short activity for students to do at the beginning of class to engage them in the lesson—these are often called "bellringers" and "do nows." Two examples of these activities that I particularly enjoy using are anticipation guides and fast writes. In an anticipation guide, students respond to a series of statements related to the day's topic by agreeing or disagreeing with each one and explaining why. These statements are designed to spark discussion, so they're most effective when they're worded in ways that encourage students to either strongly agree or disagree. Figure 3.2 depicts an anticipation

Figure 3.2 Example Anticipation Guide

Anticipation Guide: "Kim" from *Seedfolks*

Directions: Read each of the statements below. Then, write whether you agree or disagree with each one and explain why.

1. People of all sizes and ages can show bravery.
    Do you agree or disagree?

    Explanation:

2. We can make our families proud of us in many different ways.
    Do you agree or disagree?

    Explanation:

3. Believing you'll be successful is more important than having evidence.
    Do you agree or disagree?

    Explanation:

4. Children always need the help of adults when doing important things.
    Do you agree or disagree?

    Explanation:

guide I've used to prepare my students to read and discuss a section from Paul Fleischman's novel *Seedfolks* that is told from the point of view of a young girl named Kim, who braves challenging conditions in a quest to honor her father's memory. Each statement on the anticipation guide requires students to think about an important issue in the text. When creating your own anticipation guides, I recommend identifying three to five ideas related to the content of a particular lesson or activity and asking students to reflect on them by agreeing or disagreeing with each one and explain why.

Fast writes, the other activity I enjoy using at the beginning of class to help students focus on and engage with the material, involve giving students a word or phrase related to an instructional topic and asking them to write whatever comes to mind for one minute when thinking of that topic. I ask the students to write as continuously as possible and tell them that they can use any format—list, stream of consciousness, word web, or anything else that works for them. For example, if I want to build up to a reading and discussion about the pros and cons of technology, I can ask my students to do a fast write on the word "technology" and then ask for volunteers to share excerpts from their fast writes. Similarly, if I'm preparing my students for a discussion of the attributes of argument writing, I can ask them to do a fast write on the phrase "a strong argument" and then invite volunteers to share their ideas.

A Strong Sense of Pace

I've found that a well-paced lesson is crucial to managing student behavior. A lesson with a strong sense of pace is one that is fast-moving, but also accounts for the time students need to complete an assigned task or understand a key concept. When I talk with new English teachers about created well-paced lessons, I emphasize that learning activities shouldn't take any longer than they need to; activities that take longer than necessary create extra, unused time that students will often use to get off task. To get a general understanding of how long an activity needs to take, I start by asking myself "What is the main goal of this activity?" If the activity is a mini-lesson designed to remind my students of the differences between specific and general nouns, I know that goal won't take very long for my students to reach. Conversely, if I'm scheduling time for my students to apply the strategy of specific nouns to their own works, I allot more time, since it's something that will typically take students a longer time to complete.

I frequently notice the connection between pacing and classroom management when I'm observing English teachers: the teachers with the best management skills are the ones that structure the timing of their learning activities so well that students don't really have a chance to get off task. To illustrate this, let's envision two scenarios that involve teachers their students to complete a small-group activity in which they draw conclusions about characters' motivations in *The Great Gatsby*. In one situation, the teacher clearly communicates to students that they have five minutes to complete the activity. This teacher notifies the students exactly how much time they'll have, updates them on how much time remains throughout the activity, and even projects an electronic timer to the front of the room to let the students know how much time has gone by and how much is left. In the other situation, the teacher asks the students to work the activity, but does not mention anything about how much time they should take on it. As the students work, the teacher makes statements like "Everyone should be working right now" and "Finish up soon," but does not make any concrete statements about how much time has been allotted for the activity and how much of that time remains.

I've observed classroom activities resembling both of these scenarios: situations in which an activity was well-paced with an appropriate amount of time allotted and the number of remaining minutes clearly communicated, as well as those in which there is little to no sense of pacing or communication of the amount of time scheduled for the activity. In the well-paced activities where the timing expectations were made clear, student behavior was far more on task than in those activities in which the pacing and scheduling were more nebulous. An effectively paced class, in which activities are timed appropriately and that time clearly communicated to students, makes a huge difference in classroom management.

A Thorough Lesson Plan

I think of a thorough lesson plan as having two key components: learning activities that take up the whole class period and variation in those activities. Each one of these components is important to keeping students engaged and maximizing classroom management. Having enough learning activities to fill the entire instructional period is essential to keeping students on task: whenever I've underestimated the amount of activities needed for a class period, I either finished my instruction early (which left me scrambling to find something for students to do until the bell rang) or tried to make activities in my plan take longer (which resulted in students getting off task during those unnecessarily lengthy activities, such as in the *Gatsby* activity discussed in the previous section). These experiences taught me the importance of having in a lesson plan at least enough activities to fill one class period (and sometimes more if I was unsure how long certain activities would take). If I ran out of time for an activity with my students on one day, I could move the activity to the next class or omit it if I felt my students mastered the content to the point where they didn't need the activity. Having a thorough plan with at least enough activities to fill a class period gives me a feeling of security that I'll always have something for my students to do to stay engaged in the lesson, which maximizes their learning and my classroom management.

Varying the structure of the learning activities we give our students is also important to having a well-managed classroom. For example, I could plan an extremely detailed lesson on key ideas in *The Catcher in the Rye*, but if that lesson is just me lecturing, I'll lose my students' attention and will certainly have some classroom management issues. Instead, a much more effective lesson plan would incorporate a number of components, such as a mini-lesson, an interactive discussion, and a small-group or individual application of the concept. A lesson with all of these components would engage students in a variety of ways, giving variety to the class period and providing students with a number of opportunities to learn and interact with the material.

Clear organization, a strong sense of pace, and a thorough lesson plan are important components of effective instruction and strong classroom management: instruction that incorporates these features increases the likelihood that students will remain focused and on-task. In the next section, we'll take a look inside a ninth-grade classroom and see how I use these instructional procedures to help maximize my classroom management.

What Does It Look Like in Action?

"For our first activity today," I tell my ninth graders, "I'd like for you to do a fast write on the word 'power.' When I ask you to begin, please take one minute and write what comes to your mind when you think of that word. You can write anything at all that you think of; just try to write as continuously as you can for that minute. Does everyone have something to write with and write on?"

The students nod and I ask them to begin. The classroom is full of the students' focused looks and non-stop pencil motions; I walk around the room, praising their efforts. "Great job, everyone," I remark. "I love how hard you all are working." The students continue to work; I comment when thirty seconds remain, then again when ten are left, and finally when the minute is up.

"I'm thrilled by how everyone worked for the whole time," I tell the class. "Now, who wants to share with the rest of us a highlight from your fast write?"

Student hands shoot up around the room. I first call on a student who states, "One thing I said is that power is all about influence."

Another explains, "I said power means getting what you want, whatever that means for you and however you do it."

Yet another student explains, "To me, power is strength. It can be the strength of your body, of your mind, of your personality, or another kind, but it's all some type of strength."

As each student shares, I jot down a summary of the response on the whiteboard. For the first response, I write "influence"; for the second, "getting what you want"; and for the third, "strength in some form."

"Fantastic work on those responses," I tell the students. "Now, let's talk about why I asked you do that fast write. The book you started reading yesterday, *The Chocolate War* (Cormier, 1974), deals with the issue of power in a number of ways. For homework, you read the first three chapters in the book. Right now, we're going to do an activity related to the issue of power in those chapters. I'm going to give you a graphic organizer to complete in groups that asks you identify three quotations from the text and to indicate what you can infer from each quotation about the distribution of power in the scenario." (The graphic organizer used for this activity is depicted in Figure 3.3 and in Appendix A.)

"Before we get started," I tell the students, "I'll model an example so that you know exactly what's expected. I found the quotation 'Obie waited in anticipation, hating the thing that made him look at Archie in admiration. The way Archie could turn people on. Or off' (p. 12). I'll write this quotation in the top left column of the page. Now, on the top right column, I'll write what I can infer about power in this scenario. I'm going to write, 'Obie doesn't like how manipulative Archie is, but he wants to have Archie's ability to manipulate. Obie's desire to have Archie's ability gives Archie power over him.'"

Figure 3.3 Graphic Organizer for Power Analysis Activity

Quotation from Text	What You Can Infer about Power in the Scenario

"Do you all feel like you're ready to do this activity with your group members?" I ask. Students' heads nod; as they work, I move around the classroom, thrilled by how focused they are on the task. I sit down with each student group and check in on its progress, praising particularly insightful observations and making suggestions when appropriate. While the groups work, I periodically make note of the time remaining on the timer projected to the front of the room and remind the students that each group will share one of its quotations and inferences when the timer goes off. These reminders seem to help focus the students during the moments that some of their attentions appear to wander.

Once the timer sounds to indicate the end of the activity, I ask each group to share a highlight from its work. There are a number of insightful examples; one group identifies a line describing a football coach—"He growled and swore and was merciless" (p. 9)—as representative of the coach's power over his team, explaining, "This description shows the coach's powerful personality and implies the power he has with his players." Another group thoughtfully explains that a passage discussing the pain that Jerry, the book's protagonist, is willing to endure to make the football team conveys the power that football has in Jerry's life and in the lives of many high school students: "We picked out this part on page seven, 'As he turned to take the ball, a dam burst against the side of his head and a hand grenade shattered his stomach,' as showing a lot about power in the book," asserts a student. "Since it's about Jerry playing football and how much pain he felt, it shows how much power football has over him. Our group also talked about how this is true for lots of other kids our age."

As this section of the class concludes, I praise the students' excellent focus and strong academic work, noting that these two things complemented each other nicely: "Wonderful job, all of you, on these activities. You were so focused during the fast write and during the group activity. In addition, the quality of the work you did was excellent: your fast write responses were insightful and your group work identifications and inferences were thoughtful and indicative of really in-depth thinking. Great job on your outstanding focus and excellent work!"

Key Tips

In this section, we'll look closely at two key suggestions that can help you effectively incorporate the instructional ideas described in this chapter. To best understand and make use of the connection between instructional procedures and student behavior, I recommend that teachers 1) prioritize student work time and 2) use movement as a classroom management tool. Let's consider each of these suggestions by thinking about what each one means and why it can be beneficial.

1. Prioritize student work time.

When planning learning activities with both academic achievement and classroom management in mind, I strongly recommend making student work time a primary component of your instructional planning. In this context, "student work time" refers to time in the class period devoted to students applying an academic skill they have learned or are in the process of learning. For example, in a lesson on strong verbs, a teacher could conduct a brief mini-lesson devoted to explaining the attributes of strong verbs, showing students examples, and discussing the importance of this concept. Then, the majority of the time in the lesson would be devoted to the students applying this concept to their own pieces of writing by either revising something they've already written with strong verbs in mind or focusing on using strong verbs in new work. After the students have done this, a relatively brief amount of time at the end of the lesson could be devoted to students sharing the strong verbs they incorporated into their work.

In this planning format, approximately 75% of the lesson focuses on students applying a concept, while the other 25% is divided between the opening mini-lesson and the concluding share time. When I recently talked with a group of new English teachers about this idea, one expressed concern that devoting more in-class time to students working minimized the teacher's role: "The teacher doesn't seem to matter as much in this format," she stated. "It seems like it's harder for the teacher to have an impact."

"I get where you're coming from," I explained. "But this method of instruction actually gives the teacher an extremely important role: a role that has just as much, if not even more, of a chance to make an impact as other types of instruction that involve more teacher talk. It gives teachers more of a chance to talk with students individually about how they're applying the day's focal concept to their own works. After the mini-lesson, the teacher can circulate around the classroom, holding individual meetings or conferences with students to assess their understandings and give them any extra support they need." (Strategies for holding successful conferences are discussed in detail in Chapter Seven of this book).

In addition to providing opportunities for individualized instruction, this format is beneficial because of the focus it puts on student work: since most of the time is dedicated to the students working, this structure communicates to students that the work they do in class matters. When speaking with new English teachers about this benefit, I challenged them to consider the implicit messages built into their instructional decisions: "Everything we do as teachers sends a message to students: the way we structure the seating in our classroom, the writing assignments we give, the books we ask them to read, and anything else we can think of. If we teachers talk the whole class period, we're sending the message that what the teacher has to say is most important. If we devote a lot of time to students working, we send the message that we prioritize their work." Prioritizing student work also sends an important classroom management message: because it's important to us teachers that students have time to do their work, it should be important to the students to focus on doing this work.

2. Use movement as a classroom management tool.

To maximize the effectiveness of the instructional practices and suggestions described in this chapter, I recommend moving around the classroom to enhance your classroom management and complement your instruction. I've found this to be an important tactic for keeping students focused and on task. For example, when I ask students to do an opening-of-class activity such as an anticipation guide or fast write, I move around the classroom, checking on their progress and sending the message that I value them working hard on the activity. Purposeful movement around the classroom can play an important role in every activity you ask your students to do, whether it's one of these opening tasks, small group work, a partner discussion, or an independent application of a concept.

I've found that many students regard a teacher's movement as a representation of how much she or he is involved in the lesson. An eighth-grade student I taught once told me that he really noticed how present I was in the classroom: "You really move around a lot when you teach. Whenever I was working and looked up, you were somewhere different, talking to a different [student]." This student continued to note that he felt my continued movement contributed to the success of the lesson: "You moving around like that keeps everyone on their toes, keeps them working hard. No one messed around." As this student's comments suggest, moving purposefully around the classroom while students work is a way to communicate to students how important their work is to you—and, by extension, should be to them. It's similar in many ways to the previous recommendation about scheduling a significant amount of time for student work: it sends a message that you value the work your students are doing and want them to do as well. My response to the eighth-grader who commented on me moving around the classroom indicates why I feel this practice is important: "I'm glad you noticed. I want to show you all that I care about your work, and one way I can show that is by moving around and checking on how you and your classmates are doing while you all are working."

Final Thoughts on Understanding the Connection between Instructional Procedures and Student Behavior

◆ Classroom management skills and instructional abilities are sometimes considered to be two totally separate aspects of a teacher's skill set, but I believe they're very closely related.

- Having a clearly organized, well-paced, and thorough lesson plan is essential to strong classroom management.
  - Clear organization is present when there is a structured lesson plan for students to follow that includes a posted agenda and a clearly communicated procedure for students to follow at the beginning of class.
  - A strong sense of pace is present when a lesson moves relatively briskly, while still allowing for students to have enough time needed to complete the tasks.
  - A thorough lesson plan is one that includes many varied learning activities so that students are engaged in a number of ways. There isn't any empty time at the end of a class period or a need to make activities take longer than they should.
- Clear organization is important to effective classroom management because organized instructional procedures communicate to students that they're in an environment where learning is taken seriously and that they are expected to behave in ways that are conducive to learning.
- A strong sense of pace is important to classroom management because well-timed learning activities don't give students have a chance to get off task.
- A thorough lesson plan is important to effective management because the combination of learning activities that take up the whole class period and variation in those activities keeps students active and engaged throughout the class period.
- To maximize the connection between instructional procedures and student behavior, I recommend keeping the following recommendations in mind, as they will help create a well-run classroom that focuses on student productivity:
  - Prioritize student work time.
  - Use movement as a classroom management tool.

4

Integrate Technology Purposefully

In this chapter, we'll examine a crucial aspect of English instruction today: how to incorporate technological purposefully and strategically. First, we'll consider what it means to purposefully integrate technologically into English instruction and then reflect on why doing so is important to effective teaching. After that, we'll look at a description of how I put this idea into action with a ninth-grade English class. Finally, we'll examine some key recommendations to help you purposefully integrate technology in your instruction.

What Is It?

It seems like every time I visit a school, attend an educational conference, or talk with a group of teachers, I learn about a new technological innovation that can be incorporated into my English instruction. When I hear about these programs, apps, and other potential multimedia integrations, I'm often conflicted: on one hand, I know that multimedia has the potential to make English class more relevant, engaging, and authentic for students (Wolsey & Grisham, 2012). On the other hand, however, I also know that technology is sometimes used excessively and is integrated for the sake of doing so, not because it's the best way to achieve an instructional objective (Young & Bush, 2004).

I've learned to address this challenge by looking at each technological innovation with a critical eye, carefully evaluating whether or not using it would make a positive impact on the learning that takes place in my classroom. To determine if a form of technology is worth using, I ask myself a key question: "How can using this technology in my classroom improve student learning?" If I am able to identify a way that the technological innovation can do so, it has merit and is worth incorporating into my instruction. Asking and answering this question is an essential aspect of purposefully integrating technology into the English classroom. Teachers who carefully consider if a technological innovation can enhance their students' learning are looking at these innovations through a critical lens and not simply using technology without regard for the impact it has on their students. In the next section, we'll consider why purposefully integrating technology is important to effective English instruction.

Why Does It Matter?

The purposeful integration of technology enhances English instruction in a variety of ways: it prioritizes student learning, eliminates the frustration of excessive technology use, and helps students become careful technology users. In this section, we'll explore each of these benefits of strategically incorporating technology, reflecting on how its purposeful use leads to each one and why each enhances the experiences of both students and teachers.

Prioritizes Student Learning

Strategically approaching technology use sends a message to students that their learning is the main focus of what's taking place in the classroom. To illustrate this, let's take a look at an example: I was recently working with a seventh-grade English class that featured a lot of shy students who were reluctant to share their ideas in class discussion, but they had excellent insights that would contribute to the learning of everyone in the class. Since online discussion boards are excellent ways to expand participation opportunities in class discussions (traditional discussions favor vocal extroverts and those who require less think-time before commenting) (Grisham & Wolsey, 2006), I decided to use this technological integration to provide more opportunities for students to comfortably share their ideas and therefore learn from each other. With this goal in mind, I brought in the laptop cart one day and asked the students to comment on several discussion questions and one another's insights instead of having a face-to-face discussion. The conversation went very well—a wide range of students contributed to the conversation and commented thoughtfully on others' insights.

It's important to note that I didn't replace face-to-face discussions with these online discussion board activities, but instead occasionally incorporated the discussion boards to provide a variation on the traditional classroom conversation. The most significant aspect of this particular technology integration is that I did it to enhance the learning experiences of my students. When making decisions about technological forms to integrate into your classes, consider the needs you feel the students have and reflect on which technology tools would best help meet those needs. For example, if your students could benefit from being able to review your mini-lessons when studying for tests, you might consider recording them and posting them online for the students to access. What's most important isn't what specific technological form you use but rather that you've selected that type of technology based on what your students' needs are.

Eliminates the Frustration of Excessive Technology Use

Another benefit of the strategic integration of technology is that it eliminates the feelings of frustration and burnout that come with the excessive use of technological devices in the classroom. Recent conversations I've had with students and teachers indicate that using technological tools in every possible situation does more harm than good; a high-school English teacher recently explained, "Using tech is definitely a double-edged sword: it can be great if you use it at just the right time, but it can be a disaster if you use it too much. If everything you do as a teacher uses technology, you start to rely on it too much and you and your students don't get certain benefits." This teacher continued to explain that she felt her students' abilities to collaborate suffered when she reduced the amount of time they worked together in person in favor of technological innovations that streamlined the collaborative process: "I thought I was being efficient, but I was really depriving my students of the important experience of person-to-person collaboration. They got bored working together on [a technological platform] instead of in person, and their work suffered, too. I've learned to think more carefully about how and why I use technology."

I was intrigued that the high-school students with whom I spoke shared the belief that an overuse of technology can hinder the learning experience. One student asserted, "It can be helpful sometimes when teachers use technology, like when they post due dates online so you can double-check when an assignment is due, or when you can use it to do something fun, like creating a video about something you learned, but it can get really boring if the teachers use it too much." When asked what "too much" can look like, the student explained, "Like, I had a teacher that had us use technology to answer every question about what we read: we would click the button that went with the answer we thought was right, and that was it. We didn't really discuss things." Another student in the same class recalled an English class in middle school that overused student laptops: "We had these laptops in seventh-grade English, and we used them all the time. We would read articles and stories on the laptops and then answer questions on the laptops and the teacher would get the answers sent to her through a program. That was pretty much the class. It would have been a lot more fun if we did other things and didn't use the laptops so much."

What stands out to me most about these students' insights and the teacher's comments in the preceding paragraph is the idea that technology is best used purposefully as a tool that complements English instruction—an idea reflected in key research on the topic (Pasternak, 2007; Pope & Golub, 2000). The students' statements suggest that technology resources are valuable when used with particular goals in mind, such as accessing information easily or creating an interactive and enjoyable way for students to express their knowledge, but can also make for ineffective teaching if overused. Using technology to meet specific instructional goals—not simply to meet the goal of using technology—guards against the potential downfalls this teacher and these students identify.

Helps Students Become Careful Technology Users

As teachers, we model so many important behaviors for our students; just as our students can benefit from seeing us teachers as active and engaged readers and writers (Fletcher & Portalupi, 2001), they can become strategic and careful technology users if we show them what this looks like. I recently explained this belief to an eighth-grade English class I was teaching: "If I ask you to use technology," I explained, "I'm going to do it because that form of technology is the best way to reach the learning goal we're trying to achieve together. For example, I'm going to ask you to go online and look up articles on environmental issues that you can then compare to the environmental issues in *California Blue* (Klass, 1994), which is the next novel we're going to read together." (This novel addresses the tension between protecting a new butterfly species and maintaining the logging industry in the town in which the butterfly is found.) "When I ask you to go online and find these articles," I continued, "I'll be doing so because I think it's the best way to reach the learning goal of comparing the events in this novel with real-world environmental issues—not just because I want you to use the Internet more."

While it's amusing to think that a teacher would give students assignments just to have them using the Internet more, it's important to consider the impact that technology use in the classroom can have on students' perceptions of it. Instruction in which technology seems to be used as much as possible, with little consideration of whether or not it's the best way to reach a particular learning goal, can send a message to students that technology should be used in every situation. Conversely, instruction that uses technology purposefully, with clear explanations given to students about why a particular form of technology is used and what learning goal it's helping the class reach, can send the message that technological innovations are tools to use purposefully and carefully. Given the prevalence of technology in today's world, it's easy for students to become reliant on technological programs in every aspect of their lives. If we teachers use our instruction to model careful and strategic uses of technology, we'll provide our students with a framework for purposeful technology use that they can apply to their lives in a variety of ways.

Each of these benefits of purposeful technology use shows the positive impact that strategically incorporating technology can have on our instruction and our students' learning experiences. In the next section, we'll take a look inside a ninth-grade English class and examine how I helped my students integrate technology into their writing in a specific and purposeful way.

What Does It Look Like in Action?

"Think about the last time you read an article online," I tell my ninth graders. "Was it just text, or did it have other features in it, too?"

"There were definitely other things than just text," a student quickly responds. "There were pictures and some even had graphs and videos."

"How about the rest of you?" I continue, addressing the rest of the class. "Are there times when you've read articles and noticed features other than the text?"

Students around the classroom nod; a chorus of "yeah" and "definitely" fills the room.

"Today," I explain, "we're going to work on doing this in the argument essays we're writing. I'm going to ask you to brainstorm and then search online for images that you could use to support the claim you're making in your argument essay. The key to doing this successfully is being strategic with your choices: make sure that any images you include clearly and effectively support the claim of your essay. For example, let's say you're writing an essay that argues for the importance of public libraries and your major argument is that libraries are important because they provide children whose families can't afford a lot of books a way to still access texts that will maximize their literacy skills and their chances of being successful in school. You might select pictures of children reading different kinds of books to show the wide range of resources they can find in the library. That picture would be closely aligned with, and supportive of, the main argument of your essay. Now, imagine instead that you chose to include a picture of the beautiful architecture of a really nice library; this would be a good-looking picture, but it wouldn't do anything to support your essay. Does that make sense?"

Students around the classroom voice their understanding, so I continue: "To get you started thinking about using images in your argument essay, I'm going to ask you to work individually to find two images: one that directly relates to the main point of the argument you're making in the essay, and another that relates to the general topic of the essay, but not to the specific argument you're making. The example I just described about images of children reading can help guide you: photos of children reading a wide range of books would support the essay's main point, while an image of a library's fancy architecture wouldn't align with this point. To help you work on this activity, I'm going to give you a graphic organizer that asks you to list your essay's main argument, describe each image you find, and explain why each image is or is not aligned with your essay's argument."

I give each student a copy of this graphic organizer (depicted in Figure 4.1 and available in reproducible form in Appendix A) and ask them to get started, circulating around the classroom and checking in with them as they do.

I first check in with a student who is writing an essay that argues that high schools should eliminate tackle football and participate in flag football instead. "I'm impressed by how much you've written on your graphic organizer," I begin. "Talk to me about what you've found."

"For the image that relates to the topic but doesn't support the argument, I wrote about a picture of a football. I picked this image because it's relevant to the essay in a really general way, but doesn't have anything to do with my argument that high school students should play flag football instead of tackle."

"Great explanation," I reply. "How about the image that supports your argument?"

"For that part," responds the student, "I chose two images. One is of a helmet-to-helmet collision in a football game and the other is an image that compares how a brain looks after a concussion with the way a normal brain looks. These pictures support my argument because they show what

Figure 4.1 Graphic Organizer for Argument Essay Image Analysis

Topic	Your Response
Your essay's argument	
Description of an image related to your essay's topic that does not support your argument	
Why this image does not support your essay's argument	
Description of an image related to your essay's topic that supports your argument	
Why this image supports your essay's argument	

tackle football can do to someone: players can get hit in the head, and that can mess up their brains."

"Excellent job of describing those images and how they align with your argument," I say. "You explained the connection between those images and the points in your essay very well. I can really tell that you picked these images carefully and with a clear understanding of how they go along with the argument your essay is making."

I continue around the room, checking in with the other students in the class and finding myself similarly impressed with their careful distinction between images that generally relate to their topics and those that specifically align with their arguments. After speaking with each student individually, I address the class as a whole: "Wonderful work today, all of you. The key to the activity you did today was using technology purposefully. When you bring a picture—or any other kind of multimedia—into an argument essay, you want to bring in something that really supports your argument, not just something that's generally related to your topic. Each of you did a great job of thinking carefully about the differences between images that specifically support the argument your essay is making and those that are just related to the topic. As we keep working on these essays, I encourage you to include an image that supports your essay's claim."

Key Tips

In this section, we'll look in-depth at two key suggestions that can help you purposefully integrate technology into your English instruction as effectively as possible: 1) identify and evaluate the benefits of each technological integration you consider and 2) explain to students the benefits of each technological integration you select. These suggestions can guide you as you integrate technology into your instruction in meaningful and strategic ways. Let's consider these recommendations by reflecting on what each one means and why it can be beneficial.

1. Identify and evaluate the benefits of each technological integration you consider.

This suggestion has two related components, both important to the purposeful integration of technology into English instruction: the identification of the benefits associated with each form of technology integration you consider and the evaluation of how those benefits can enhance student learning. It's important to consider both components in order to make careful decisions about the technology we use in our instruction. I recently told a group of new English teachers that it's not enough to identify the benefit of a technological integration; to use technology effectively, we must also evaluate how helpful that benefit actually is: "A lot of people use technology just because it has *some* benefit, but that's not enough for us or for our students. We need to look carefully at each benefit and analyze how much that benefit will actually improve our teaching and our students' learning."

The graphic organizer depicted in Figure 4.2 provides a framework to use when reflecting on the benefits of particular uses of technology in English instruction; it asks for the specific way technology will be used, the key benefits associated with that use, and how those benefits can enhance student learning.

By identifying how we'll use a technological form, considering the benefits it has, and reflecting on the ways those can benefits can enhance the learning experiences of our students, we can ensure that we're using technology with our students' learning in mind.

A benefit of using this graphic organizer is that you have an instant and easy-to-create rationale for using technology that you believe to be beneficial to your students' learning. For example, recall the activity of asking students to use an online discussion board that I described earlier in this chapter. If someone challenged me on that technology use (or just wanted to know more about why I was using it), I could easily produce the graphic organizer containing my belief that this activity is beneficial because of the way it provides students with options to participate that go beyond traditional, teacher-led discussions, as well as my assertion that those benefits can enhance student learning by allowing more students to share their thoughts with the class and providing more processing time to

Figure 4.2 Graphic Organizer for Evaluating Technology Use

Component	Your Response
The specific way technology will be used	
Key benefits associated with using technology in this way	
How these benefits can enhance student learning	

those who need it. This document would illustrate that I've thought carefully about this technological form and given special consideration to how it will make a positive impact on my students' learning, showing that I'm using this technological integration for strong pedagogical reasons and not just for the sake of using technology.

2. Explain to students the benefits of each technological integration you select.

Once you've identified and analyzed the benefits of a technological integration, you'll be in a good position to determine whether you'd like to incorporate it into your instruction. When you decide on a form of technology to include in your teaching, I recommend explaining to students why you've selected that technological innovation and why you think it can be beneficial to their learning. Doing this has two key benefits: it shows students you're using technology purposefully in your instruction (thereby modeling strategic technology use) and allows them to focus on that benefit as they work.

I put this recommendation into action when working with a middle school English class on using infographics to explain key ideas in informational writing. When I introduced the concept of infographics to them and encouraged them to use them in their informational essays to compare information or highlight important facts, I explained why I felt including these features in their works could enhance their learning experiences and the quality of their works: "I wouldn't ask you to consider including infographics in your informational writings unless I thought doing so would have significant benefits. One of the major benefits of incorporating infographics is that it highlights important information in your essay and clearly communicates those points to the reader. Depending on your essay, your infographic might compare information, provide a timeline, or show a change over time. No matter which one of these purposes it serves, the infographic will communicate especially important information to readers very clearly."

"In addition," I continued, "using infographics to highlight important details can also enhance your learning: when you create an infographic that conveys key information to your reader, you're forced to look carefully at the facts in your essay that you discovered in your research and identify which ones are most important and why. Then, you need to decide to which infographic format will best align with this information. It's a great way to make sure you understand the material in your essay; if you're able to clearly and effectively create an infographic about important information in your essay, you definitely have a strong understanding of the key details in the piece."

Highlighting the benefits of the technology you use in your English instruction can also be empowering to students because it can send the message that you care enough about them to explain your instructional decisions. A student in the class that helped incorporate infographics into their informational essays remarked that he felt respected and empowered by my comments on how including this form of technology can enhance his learning: "I wish more teachers would do that," he reflected, "and say 'This is how doing this can help you learn better' and 'This is why I'm saying you should do this.' It's usually just teachers telling us to do things because they said to do them. I felt like you cared and respected us because you took the time to explain this."

Final Thoughts on Integrating Technology Purposefully

- ◆ Integrating technology purposefully involves looking at technological innovations with a critical eye, carefully evaluating whether or not using each innovation would make a positive impact on the learning that takes place in the classroom.
- ◆ To determine if a form of technology is worth using, I ask myself a key question: "How can using this technology in my classroom improve student learning?" If I am able to identify a way that the technological innovation can do so, it has merit and is worth incorporating into my instruction.
- ◆ The purposeful integration of technology enhances English instruction in a variety of ways: it prioritizes student learning, eliminates the frustration of excessive technology use, and helps students become careful technology users.
  - ◆ This practice prioritizes student learning by sending a message to students that their learning—not using technology whenever possible—is the main focus of what's taking place in the classroom.
  - ◆ It eliminates the frustration of excessive technology use by limiting the integration of technology to situations that enhance teaching and learning.
  - ◆ It helps students become careful technology users by modeling for them what the strategic and purposeful selection of technology looks like.
- ◆ When strategically integrating technology into your instruction, keep these recommendations in mind because they can help you incorporate technological innovations as purposefully and effectively as possible:
  - ◆ Identify and evaluate the benefits of each technological integration you consider.
  - ◆ Explain to students the benefits of each technological integration you select.

Section 2

Assessment Strategies

5

Use Assignment-Specific Rubrics

In this chapter, we'll look carefully at an important component of evaluating student work: the effective use of assignment-specific rubrics. We'll begin by considering what assignment-specific rubrics are (and how they differ from criteria-referenced rubrics, with which they are frequently compared). Next, we'll consider how assignment-specific rubrics can benefit both students and teachers. After that, we'll look at a description of how I discussed an assignment-specific rubric with a ninth-grade English class. We'll then conclude with key recommendations for putting this idea into action in your own instruction.

What Is It?

Assignment-specific rubrics are evaluation tools that are based on the specific features of particular assignments (Bratcher & Ryan, 2004). They vary from one assignment to the next based on information such as the genre in which students are writing, the specific instructions they've been given, and the information they've been taught. Assignment-specific rubrics are frequently compared with criteria-referenced rubrics, which evaluate student work on general criteria of good writing or strong work and don't change from one assignment to the next (Bratcher & Ryan, 2004). Criteria-referenced rubrics are often based on the evaluation criteria used for state writing assessments or school-wide evaluations. Figure 5.1 highlights

Figure 5.1 Comparison between Assignment-Specific and Criteria-Referenced Rubrics

Features of Assignment-Specific Rubrics	Features of Criteria-Referenced Rubrics
◆ Vary from one assignment to the next ◆ Based on genre in which students are writing, the instruction they've been given, and the information they've been taught	◆ Stay the same across different assignments ◆ Based on general evaluation criteria for large-scale assignments such as state writing assessments or school-wide evaluations

some key distinctions between assignment-specific and criteria-referenced rubrics.

To further illustrate the features of assignment-specific rubrics and how they differ from criteria-referenced versions, let's take a look at an example of each one. Figure 5.2 depicts an assignment-generated rubric I've used when evaluating eighth-graders' performances on argument essays. The components of this rubric are based on the features of a high-quality argument essay; features such as clearly stating a claim, supporting that claim with evidence, and acknowledging and refuting potential counterclaims are essential to an effective piece of argument writing. Note that there are some components of this rubric, such as mechanics and supporting details, that would also show up on a rubric for pieces written in other genres or on a criterion-referenced rubric. This is perfectly normal, since there is often some commonality across the different genres and assignments we examine with our students.

In contrast, a criteria-referenced rubric for the same assignment would address criteria that can be applied to a variety of genres and assignments. For example, a rubric based on the six traits of writing (Culham, 2003) would evaluate a piece on the traits of ideas, voice, organization, word choice, sentence fluency, and conventions. Figure 5.3 depicts a rubric that could be used for a criteria-referenced evaluation based on these six traits. (Reproducible versions of Figures 5.2 and 5.3 are available in Appendix A.)

A criteria-referenced rubric could address other evaluation components than these, but wouldn't be specifically geared to the features and components of a particular assignment like the argument writing rubric in Figure 5.2. Instead, it would address general features of effective writing that are not aligned with specific genres or tasks.

Now that we've examined the attributes of assignment-specific rubrics and how they compare to criteria-referenced versions, let's consider why assignment-specific rubrics are important to successful assessments.

Figure 5.2 Assignment-Specific Rubric for an Argument Essay

Component	Evaluation Criteria	Possible Points	Your Score
Introducing claims	◆ Does the introductory paragraph effectively communicate to readers the issue the rest of the piece will be describing? ◆ Does the author clearly communicate his or her position on this issue?	4	
Acknowledging alternate or opposing claims	◆ Does the piece clearly incorporate an alternate or opposing view that differs from the author's claim? ◆ Does the piece include information that refutes this alternate or opposing claim?	4	
Organizing reasons and evidence logically	◆ Are the essay's paragraphs clearly divided into separate ideas? ◆ Are the paragraphs sequenced in a logical way, such as beginning with an introduction, moving to paragraphs that support the piece's claim, transitioning to discussions of alternate or opposing claims, and then finishing with a concluding section?	4	
Creating an effective concluding section	◆ Does the conclusion emphasize the significance of the cause for which the essay is arguing? ◆ Does the conclusion leave readers with a final thought about the piece's claim?	4	

Figure 5.2 Continued

Component	Evaluation Criteria	Possible Points	Your Score
Supporting details	◆ Are the ideas and insights in the essay supported by relevant details that clearly relate to the points they are supporting?	4	
Strong mechanics	◆ Does the piece demonstrate an understanding of proper punctuation? ◆ Are sentences clear and representative of complete thoughts? ◆ Is capitalization used at appropriate times?	4	

This rubric is adapted from my book *The Argument Writing Toolkit* (Ruday, 2016).

Figure 5.3 Example of Criteria-Referenced Rubric

Component	Evaluation Criteria	Possible Points	Your Score
Ideas	◆ Is the piece's central idea clear? ◆ Is the idea supported with relevant details?	4	
Voice	◆ Is there a clear sense of voice to the piece? ◆ Is it clear what the author wants the reader to feel?	4	
Organization	◆ Is the piece structured in a logical way? ◆ Are the sections of the piece organized based on common characteristics? ◆ Do these sections convey meaning with their order?	4	

Figure 5.3 Continued

Component	Evaluation Criteria	Possible Points	Your Score
Word choice	◆ Does the piece include a variety of vocabulary? ◆ Does the piece use specific language that aligns with the intended meaning?	4	
Sentence fluency	◆ Does the piece include a range of sentence constructions (such as simple, compound, and complex sentences)? ◆ Are these sentence constructions used in ways that align with the information the author is attempting to convey?	4	
Conventions	◆ Does the author demonstrate a mastery of capitalization, punctuation, and spelling?	4	

Why Does It Matter?

The use of assignment-specific rubrics allows for the maximum amount of nuance and detail in our evaluation of student work. This assessment method is important to effective instruction for two important, related reasons: it helps instruction and assessment align, and it accounts for differences in distinct genres and assignments. Let's examine each of these ideas individually.

Assignment-Specific Rubrics Help Connect Assessment and Instruction

Connecting assessment and instruction is a key feature of effective evaluation (Bratcher & Ryan, 2004). Since teachers who use assignment-specific evaluations create distinct rubrics for different writing assignments, they can easily craft rubrics that directly correspond with what they've taught their students in preparation for each assignment. For example, the argument-essay rubric depicted in Figure 5.2 contains the attributes of strong argument writing that I addressed in my instruction. Because I taught my students about these concepts and then evaluated their work on those attributes, I ensured that my instruction and assessment were closely linked. One student who completed this assignment scored highly on all aspects of the rubric except for the section on acknowledging alternate or opposing claims, which showed me that the student understood all of the argument-writing related strategies I taught except for that one. In my follow-up instruction with this student, I addressed ways to effectively and convincingly address alternate or opposing claims and why doing so is important to effective argument writing. If my rubric wasn't closely linked with the instruction I delivered, I wouldn't have learned so much about how well this student understood the concepts I taught him and his classmates. Since I developed such an in-depth understanding of this student's strengths and weaknesses and used this information to inform my future instruction, I was able to help this student improve: later in the school year, he wrote another argument essay and did a fantastic job of addressing claims that could be made by his opposition!

Assignment-Specific Rubrics Account for Differences in Genres and Assignments

This benefit of assignment-specific rubrics extends from the previous one: one reason these rubrics facilitate the alignment of instruction and assessment is that they reflect the differences in specific genres and assignments. For example, the same students writing the previously described argument essay also wrote poems that focused on meaningful events in their lives. When assessing the students' poems, I used a rubric that corresponded with this assignment; the components of this rubric align with the features of the genre of poetry and with the specific attributes of the project. (This rubric is depicted in Figure 5.4 and in Appendix A.)

Figure 5.4 Event-Focused Poetry Rubric

Component	Evaluation Criteria	Possible Points	Your Score
Focus	◆ Does the poem clearly focus on a singular event in the speaker's life?	4	
Detail	◆ Is the event described in detail? ◆ Do the descriptive details used make it easy for readers to understand the key components of the event?	4	

Figure 5.4 Continued

Component	Evaluation Criteria	Possible Points	Your Score
Concrete language	◆ Does the poem use concrete language, such as specific nouns and strong verbs? ◆ Is the concrete language relevant to the poem and used in a way that contributes to readers' understandings of it?	4	
Stanzas	◆ Does the poem contain at least two stanzas? ◆ Are the stanzas organized purposefully in ways that correspond with distinct aspects of the poem?	4	
Message	◆ Does the poem deliver a clear message about why the event is significant to the speaker's life?	4	

Without such a specific, assignment-focused rubric, I would not have been able to assess the students' works in such direct ways. A criteria-referenced such as the one in Figure 5.3 that addresses the attributes of strong writing in general ways would provide assessment information, but that data would be much more general than what the assignment-specific rubric conveys.

As the ideas and examples described in this section explain, assignment-specific rubrics function as key tools for effective English instruction by facilitating the connection between instruction and assessment and accounting for differences in distinct genres and assignments. I strongly recommend creating rubrics for your students that align with the specific assignments you give them; this will provide your students with clear expectations that increase their chances of success and give you specific, useful assessment data. In the next section, we'll take a look at how I helped a class of ninth graders understand the features of an assignment-specific rubric.

What Does It Look Like in Action?

My ninth graders have recently returned from a field trip to Washington, DC, that focused on visiting and studying the iconic monuments there.

Building off their experiences on this trip, I'm asking the students to write informational essays about a monument we visited during the trip. Each student is to select a monument of her or his choice, research it, and create a piece of informational writing that discusses its history, features, and significance. The students and I have been studying informational writing in preparation for their work on this assignment by examining mentor texts and highlighting what makes them effective.

Today's a very important day to the students' success on this assignment: I'm going to talk with them about what should be on an assignment-specific rubric that evaluates their performance on the informational pieces they're writing. "We've been talking a lot about informational writing," I remind them at the beginning of class. "We've read informational works, discussed what makes them strong, and reflected on how we can apply these attributes to our own writing.

"Today, we're going to think further about the informational essays you'll be writing about Washington, DC, monuments," I continue. "I'd like you to take one minute and write down some characteristics you think these informational essays you're writing should possess to be effective. Think about the mentor texts I've shown you, the attributes of strong informational writing we've discussed in class, and the features of this specific assignment. Once you've written down some of these characteristics, share what you've written with a partner. Then, I'll ask for you to share your ideas with the whole class."

The students jot down their thoughts and then share those ideas with others sitting near them. While they share with their partners, I move around the classroom and listen to their comments. As I do this, I'm thrilled to hear many students talk about the standards of quality we discussed in class. One student tells her partner, "I wrote about how you really need to make sure you have strong sources because if your sources aren't legit, it can totally mess up the paper." The student's partner replies, "I wrote about having a good introduction because it gets the reader's attention and shows what you'll be writing about."

Once the students have finished sharing their responses with their partners, I call the class back together: "I heard some wonderful insights in your partner shares. Now I'm going to ask for some volunteers to share your ideas with the rest of us about what attributes the informational essays you're writing should possess. Who would like to get us started?"

The first student to share asserts that a strong sense of organization is important: "I think the essay has to be organized. If it isn't organized well, it won't make sense because it will be confusing. The essay will just kind of jump around and that will be confusing to the reader."

"Nice job of describing the importance of that attribute," I reply. "I'm going to write 'organized' on the whiteboard. Now, who else would like to share?"

Another student explains, "I said that it has to have important information about the monument you're writing about."

"Absolutely!" I exclaim, smiling. "I love that you focused on that. We've been talking about how the essay should describe the history, features, and significance of the monument, and your comment addresses that. I'm going to write 'information' on the board and write 'history, features, and significance' next to it to show the specific kinds of information to include."

Students continue to share important insights about the features a strong informational essay about this topic should possess. At the end of our discussion, I've written the following attributes on the whiteboard:

- Organized
- Information: history, features, and significance
- Introduction that gets readers' attention and shows what the essay is about
- Strong conclusion
- Reputable sources

I read these standards of quality out loud and praise the students' efforts: "Awesome job, all of you! You did such a great job of reflecting on share the features of an informational essay on a Washington, DC, monument. I like how much you focused on this specific assignment and the attributes of the informational mentor texts we examined. I'm going to use these to inform the rubric that I create for your informational essays. Then, I'll show you the rubric in class tomorrow. After that, you'll take some time in class to get started working on the essay!"

Now, let's fast forward to the next day of class. When the students enter, the rubric I created with the help of their insights is displayed on the document camera and projected to the front of the room. (This rubric is depicted in Figure 5.5 and available in Appendix A.)

Figure 5.5 Washington, DC, Monument Essay Rubric

Component	Evaluation Criteria	Possible Points	Your Score
Organization	◆ Does each one of the essay's paragraphs have a central focus? ◆ Do the paragraphs logically flow from one to the next?	4	
History	◆ Does the essay provide a detailed description of the monument's history, paying special attention to important people, events, and dates?	4	

Figure 5.5 Continued

Component	Evaluation Criteria	Possible Points	Your Score
Features	◆ Does the essay describe the monument's key features in detail, indicating that the author has an excellent understanding of these attributes?	4	
Significance	◆ Does the essay provide a detailed discussion of the monument's historical and cultural significance, including information about what the message the monument sends?	4	
Introduction	◆ Does the essay's introduction grab the reader's attention and clearly convey what the essay is about?	4	
Conclusion	◆ Does the conclusion leave readers with a final thought or message about the monument? ◆ Does it go beyond summarizing the essay's content?	4	
Sources	◆ Does the essay cite current, unbiased, and reputable sources for its information when applicable and appropriate?	4	
Mechanics	◆ Does the piece demonstrate an understanding of proper punctuation (especially when integrating quotations and outside sources into the essay)? ◆ Are sentences clear and representative of complete thoughts?	4	

I call the attention the students' attention it: "Here is the rubric I'll use to evaluate the informational essays you'll write about Washington, DC, monuments. As you can see, it's very closely based on the attributes you all shared with me during yesterday's discussion. The only evaluation component I added was a section on strong mechanics because I want you to also be focusing on that when you write. You can see that the rubric lists each of the evaluation components I'll use to assess your work, further descriptions of those components, and the number of points available for each component."

I give each student a hard copy of the rubric and give them further instructions: "Keep this rubric with you while you write the essay. Since it tells you exactly what you'll be graded on, it's a valuable tool for your success. While you write, I'll check in with you and ask how you're doing. When we confer about your progress up to that point, we'll use the rubric to guide our discussion and monitor your progress."

Before I transition to student-writing time, I conclude this part of the class with a final statement: "Again, great job all of you on generating ideas for this rubric! I'm really impressed with your insights, and I can't wait to see the essays you create!"

Key Tips

Let's consider two recommendations that can make your implementation of assignment-specific rubrics as effective as possible: 1) ask students for input on the rubric and 2) give students rubrics before they write. These suggestions can maximize the benefits of this rubric type by giving students clear expectations and engaging them in the assessment process. We'll now look at each of these suggestions in detail by exploring what they are and why they can be beneficial.

1   Ask students for input on the rubric.

When I share this recommendation with new teachers, I sometimes get surprised looks and incredulous comments. "Why would I ask students what should be on the rubric?" one asked. "Won't they just say they want really easy things to be on it?" While there is always a possibility of a student trying to do this, my experience has been that students take the job seriously when I ask them to help me create a rubric on which they'll be assessed. One way to maximize the likelihood that students approach this task with a sense of focus is to frame it as a reflective activity in which students think back on their previous instruction and the examples they've seen. They can then use these reflections to help generate standards of quality for the pieces they're creating. I used this tactic in the lesson described in the preceding section: I asked the students to think about our discussions about informational writing and the examples I showed them and use those reflections to create some ideas about what should be in the informational pieces they were preparing to write.

Note that you aren't obligated to use everything the students say in the rubric you ultimately use: in the example described in the last section, I took the students' insights and added another category to it. During other instances when I've done similar activities, I omitted some students' suggestions because they didn't represent writing attributes we had discussed. I like to explain to students why I made certain additions or omitted particular suggestions so that they continue to feel involved in and informed about the process.

In addition to helping students feel engaged and involved in the assessment, a great benefit of this practice is that it provides important insights into what the students have learned about the writing genre or assignment you'll be asking them to do. For example, if I'm preparing my students to write argument essays and I ask them what the standards of quality should be for evaluating argument writing, my hope is that they'll identify the attributes that we discussed and were present in the mentor texts we studied. If there are some major features that students don't identify, I'll conclude that I need to spend more time discussing those components before moving forward. For example, if none of my students mention the importance of supporting the essay's claim with relevant details, I'll conduct another mini-lesson on that topic and show students examples of it to ensure their understandings.

2   Give students rubrics before they write.

Once you've used the students' ideas and your own insights to create the rubrics that you'll use to evaluate your students' work on an assignment, I recommend giving your students those rubrics before they begin writing the piece. When I share rubrics with my students, I like to project the rubric to the front of the classroom using the document camera and discuss its features with them. Then, I give each student a hard copy of the rubric and suggest that they use it to guide their work as they write.

When I talk with teachers about the importance of giving students rubrics before the students begin working on an assignment, I encourage the teachers to think of specific ways they'll help their students use those rubrics to maximize their benefits. I recently explained this to a group of teachers: "Giving students rubrics before they write definitely gives them clear expectations about what we'll look for when we grade, and that's awesome," I told them. "I've found, though, that there are some things we can do as teachers to get students to really focus on these rubrics and maximize the benefit that they'll get from having them."

One of the tactics I recommend teachers employ is using the rubric to help guide the writing conferences they hold with their students. I mentioned this practice to my students in the previously described example of classroom practice, telling them that I'll use the rubric to inform our discussions and monitor their progress when talking with them about their pieces. When meeting with a student who was close to completing a first draft of her informational essay about the Martin Luther King Jr. Memorial, we looked at the rubric together and discussed what she had done well and if there was anything else she could work on. By the end of our conversation, she had concluded (and I agreed) that she done everything the rubric asked her to do, with one exception: she hadn't included much information about the specific physical features of the monument. Our rubric-enhanced conference helped her identify this area of growth and then revise the piece to include more of this information.

Another practice that can maximize the effectiveness of these rubrics is asking students to self-assess their work using the rubric. Before students turn in a final draft, I ask them to evaluate their own performance by scoring themselves on the rubric. I've found that requiring the students to use the rubric in this way helps them conduct purposeful revisions of their works; I told the students writing informational essays about monuments that having the rubric is like having a guidebook to how they're being evaluated: "Because you have the rubric I'm going to use, there should be no surprises," I told them, "but that also means you don't have any excuses. Once you finish your final draft, read it carefully next to the rubric and evaluate it based on the rubric criteria. Once you've done that evaluation, revise your work accordingly: if there's something in your piece that could be done better or expanded on, make those revisions before you turn it in."

Final Thoughts on Using Assignment-Specific Rubrics

- ◆ Assignment-specific rubrics are evaluation tools that are based on the specific features of particular assignments (Bratcher & Ryan, 2004) and vary from one assignment to the next based on genre attributes and instructional goals.
- ◆ Assignment-specific rubrics are often compared with criteria-referenced rubrics, which evaluate student work on general criteria of good writing or strong work and don't change from one assignment to the next (Bratcher & Ryan, 2004).
- ◆ The use of assignment-specific rubrics is important to effective instruction for two important, related reasons: it helps instruction and assessment align and it accounts for differences in distinct genres and assignments.
  - ◆ Assignment-specific rubrics facilitate the alignment of instruction and assessment by helping teachers craft different rubrics for each of their assignments that directly align with that they've taught students in preparation for those assignments.

- ◆ These rubrics account for the differences in distinct genres and assignments because they cater to the specific features of each of the writing assignments students complete: for example, a rubric for an argument writing assignment would evaluate students on different criteria than would one used for poetry writing.
- ◆ When implementing assignment-specific rubrics with your students, keep the following recommendations in mind, as they can maximize the benefits of this rubric type by giving students clear expectations and engaging them in the assessment process:
  - ◆ Ask students for input on the rubric.
  - ◆ Give students rubrics before they write.

6

Respond to Student Writing in Meaningful and Useful Ways

In this chapter, we'll explore an important component of English instruction: crafting written responses to student writing that are meaningful to students and facilitate their growth. First, we'll examine what it means to respond to student writing in this way and then reflect on the importance of doing so. After that, we'll check out a description of how I put this idea into action with my ninth graders. We'll then conclude by considering some key recommendations to follow when responding to your own students' writing.

What Is It?

While it's natural for us English teachers to want to give our students every suggestion we can think of to make their works as effective as possible, research (e.g., Ferris, 2007) cautions against this, instead urging teachers to provide their students with selective, personalized responses that help students continue to feel ownership of their works. I've identified three ways for teachers do this: 1) select one or two piece-specific areas of growth, 2) be sure the areas of growth are within students' abilities, and 3) use the responses to identify strengths in students' works. In this section, we'll explore each of these ideas in more detail.

Select One or Two Piece-Specific Areas of Growth
I've found that the most effective written responses to student writing are those that focus on one or two areas of growth that can make that particular piece as effective as possible. For example, I recently read a personal

narrative written by a seventh-grader about his experience volunteering at a food bank. Although the piece was quite strong, there were still several ways the student could have further enhanced it. However, in my written response to the final draft, I did not focus on each aspect of the piece that could have been better; I selected two areas of improvement that I felt were especially important to the piece's improvement: the use of sensory details and the organization of the memoir. In my comments, I explained how attention to each of these attributes could have further developed this already-strong narrative. If I had made a great many suggestions about ways the piece could have been improved, the student would likely feel overwhelmed and get the sense that I was taking control of the piece away from him. By making a couple of selective suggestions, I acknowledged the student's status as the author and positioned myself as a helpful instructor rather than an overbearing grader.

Be Sure the Areas of Growth Are within Students' Abilities

When deciding which areas of growth to highlight in your comments, it's important to keep in mind which suggestions are within students' ranges of abilities. To determine this, I reflect on which strategies students have learned and are able to apply to their own works with some guidance. For example, when responding to the previously mentioned memoir written by a seventh grader, I thought about what I had taught him and what strategies seemed to be in within his reach. I wouldn't suggest this student incorporate symbolism or allude to classical literature, as those strategies were beyond what he had learned and went past his abilities at that time. Suggesting areas of growth that are well beyond a student's current ability level and not yet addressed in his or her instruction would only lead to frustration and confusion, while making recommendations that students have studied and can grasp helps students feel that growth is within reach.

Use the Responses to Identify Strengths in Students' Works

Useful responses to student writing also highlight major strengths in the students' works, helping students understand what they've done well and how they've done it. When I identify important strengths in a student's work, I make my comments selective, specific, and relevant to the student's understandings (just as I would when noting an area that can be improved). I want my students to know what their strengths are so that they can continue to utilize those skills in their future works. When explaining the importance of knowing one's strengths to my students, I make connections to other scenarios: "If you're playing basketball, you want to know what your strengths are so that you can be sure to use those strengths," I recently told a group of students.

Figure 6.1 Tactics for Responding to Student Writing in Meaningful and Useful Ways

Tactic	Explanation
Select one or two piece-specific areas of growth	Focus your responses to you students' works on one or two areas of growth that can make a particular piece as effective as possible.
Be sure the areas of growth are within students' abilities	Suggest areas of growth that students have learned about and can apply to their own works with some guidance.
Use the responses to identify strengths in students' works	Help students understand what they've done well and how they've done it so that they can apply these areas of strength to their future works.

"For example, if you're a really good three-point shooter, you'll want to take a lot of three-point shots. When it comes to writing, if you're really good at writing detailed descriptions, you'll want to really play up the detail in your writing. Similarly, if you're good with writing dialogue, you can emphasize the dialogue in your works. I want to help you understand what you're already doing well, as well as point out things you can do even better."

Figure 6.1 identifies the three ways to respond to student writing in meaningful, useful ways and explains their major components.

In the next section, we'll explore why responding to student writing in these ways is important to effective instruction.

Why Does It Matter?

One of my favorite insights about effective writing instruction is that writing teachers should be coaches and not judges (Holaday, 1997); to me, this means that our job as teachers is to give our students feedback intended to help them improve their skills—not in order to penalize them. The idea of responding to student writing in meaningful and useful ways aligns with the coaching metaphor of writing instruction: like athletes, writers are best served by guidance that recognizes what they've done well and what they can do even better. When we give our students feedback that is focused on helping them improve, we expand their "writing toolkits"—the writing skills and strategies they understand and are able to use in their works. By developing our students' writing toolkits, we provide them with a way of looking at writing that is empowering and promotes student metacognition. We'll explore each of these benefits in this section.

Meaningful and Useful Feedback Can Empower Students

Responses to student writing that recognize what students have done well and make specific suggestions that are within students' reach can empower students: these comments show students that they already have some important writing skills and that they can add to that skill set by focusing on concepts that are within their current abilities and understandings. When students know that they've already done some things well and that their work can be even better through manageable steps, it's much easier for them to have positive attitudes about writing. Drawing a comparison to the previously mentioned coaching metaphor, I know that I'd have a better attitude about a sport if a coach recognized my skills and gave me one or two suggestions for improvement within my abilities than if he or she told me every single way I should improve. The first scenario would help me feel validated and motivated to improve, while the second would leave me feeling discouraged and overwhelmed.

For example, after I responded to the previously described narrative about a student's experiences volunteering at a food bank, he explained that the strategic feedback I gave him facilitated his improvement: "I really liked how you gave me a couple things to work on instead of telling me a ton of things to fix. In the next thing I wrote, I worked on the two things you told me to pay attention too—organization and sensory detail." The student continued to note, "When I get a teacher telling me a ton of things that should be better, I don't usually do anything about it because it's just too much. When it's a couple things, I'm like, 'Yeah, I can do that.'" I'm especially struck by the way this student explains the difference in how he responded to the suggestions I gave him and how he reacted to other, more extensive comments. His interest in acting on focused, selective recommendations speaks to the importance of this approach.

Meaningful and Useful Feedback Can Promote Student Metacognition

The feedback described in this chapter is focused on helping students understand writing strategies: those they have mastered and those that they can continue to develop their abilities to use. When we talk with our students about the writing strategies that they have demonstrated in their works and the strategies they can continue to work on, we are helping them build metacognitive understandings of the importance of writing strategies. I tell my students that writing strategies are like tools and writers are like craftspeople who create things with their tools: "An experienced writer," I recently told a group of students with which I was conferring, "has a lot of strategies in her or his 'writing toolkit,' so she or he can use all of those strategies when creating a piece, just like an experienced builder might have a lot of tools and know how to use all of those tools. A less-experienced writer hasn't accumulated as many strategies yet; however, as writers learn more strategies and get comfortable with using them, they can use those strategies in their works." When I comment on students' works, I like to focus on which strategies they've used well and some carefully selected ones that can make their pieces even better. I believe that doing so builds students' awareness of the importance of writing strategies and helps them think metacognitively about which strategies they've mastered and which ones they'll target in their future works.

Meaningful and useful feedback that provides students with clear understandings of their strengths and accessible areas of improvement can help students feel empowered as writers and develop their metacognition of writing strategies. In the next section, we'll take a look at this concept in action through a description of my experience providing specific, strategy-focused feedback on ninth-grade student writing.

What Does It Look Like in Action?

If you looked into my ninth-grade classroom on a recent day, you might have felt the need to double-check that you're in a school and not the headquarters of a food-writing magazine: my students have been writing pieces that explore the relationship between food and culture, drawing on their own personal cultures and backgrounds and using a number of mentor examples to provide guidance and inspiration. We've looked at published essays about food and culture and checked out online videos that describe how the foods and cultures of various places go together. Using these mentor texts and our class activities and discussions, each student was asked to create a piece of writing in the genre of his or her choice about a food that is significant to him or her in some way. I explained to the students that the work they create should be focused primarily on describing why the food is important to them, not on providing instructions for preparing it.

Today is an important day in our work on this concept because it's the day that the students turn in their works to be evaluated. I've told the students that I'm going to use rubrics to assess their performance and that I'll also provide a written response that identifies the piece's strengths and some ways it can be even better: "These responses are designed to help you know what writing strategies you used well in your piece and which ones you could use even more effectively to further enhance it. The comments will help you know what you should keep doing in your future works and what things you might want to do more of or pay more attention to."

One piece I receive is a thoughtful personal essay that describes how the author associates the experience of eating tacos with the chance to spend time with his grandparents. An excerpt from this piece is depicted in Figure 6.2.

In my response to this student's work, I noted a number of significant strengths: "I love your creative uses of hashtags in the title and at

Figure 6.2 Excerpt from Student's Essay about Tacos

#TacoTogetherness

In an article published in *Smithsonian Magazine* in 2012, a professor of history at the University of Minnesota named Jeffrey M. Pilcher describes the history of tacos. He explains that he believes tacos originated in silver mines in Mexico in the eighteenth century, came to the United States in the early twentieth century, and became popular with non-Mexicans in the United States in the 1950s. Tacos seem to be especially popular today: If you go Instagram on a Tuesday, you'll probably see a picture of tacos and a caption "#TacoTuesday." I think the history and popularity of tacos is interesting, but my experience with them is different and a lot more personal.

There's nothing in my family background that relates directly to tacos (we're don't have relatives from Mexico and don't typically make Mexican food), but this food is still really meaningful to me. That's because I associate tacos with my grandparents coming to visit my family and me. Whenever they come visit, usually on the day they arrive, my grandma makes tacos for my brothers and me.

Sure, I love the taste of the tacos—the seasoned meat, the crunchy shell, the tangy cheese. It's all delicious. I love the way the smell of the taco seasoning fills the house while my grandma cooks them and the fun of assembling all of the taco toppings before eating. I love the dinners where we eat them: the feeling of excitement of seeing my grandparents for the first time in a while, the questions my grandma asks, the jokes my grandpa tells, the silliness of my little brother jumping up and down and dancing around the dinner table when he should be eating because he's so excited.

What I love most about tacos isn't the flavor, the smell, or the texture. It's not the opportunity to join in on a popular Instagram hashtag and food trend. It's that they signal the excitement and love that goes along with my grandparents having come to visit.

#TacoTogetherness

the end of the piece!" I wrote to him. "I was also very impressed by the way you acknowledge the history and popularity of tacos in the first paragraph, while still differentiating that information from what they mean to you. In addition, you do a great job here of using descriptive language to relate your experience to the reader, such as vivid adjectives like 'seasoned,' 'crunchy,' and 'tangy' and strong verbs like 'fills,' all of which you use really nicely in the third paragraph. I know you've been working on this—very nice work!" I identified one key way this essay could be even better: "This already-strong piece could be even further enhanced with additional development of one idea: I would love to have known more about why tacos are such a special meal for your grandparents and you. Do they have a significance that originated somewhere? Did you ask for them a lot? The second paragraph could be developed even more with this information. Although additional discussion of this idea and the details around it could make the piece even stronger, this is still very good work!"

Key Tips

In this section, we'll look closely at two suggestions that can help you put the ideas discussed in this chapter into action with your students as effectively as possible: 1) identify specific sections of the text in your response and 2) personalize the feedback that you give to each student. By following these recommendations, you'll increase the usefulness of the feedback you give your students by presenting it as a teaching tool instead of a punitive measure. Let's explore what each of these suggestions means and why it can be beneficial.

1. Identify specific suggestions of the text in your response.

This is one of the most essential components of an effective written response to student writing: identifying specific suggestions of the student's piece when commenting on strengths and areas for improvement makes feedback as transparent and useful as possible. I know that when I was a student and received comments along the lines of "Interesting, but needs more detail," I was frustrated by the lack of specificity. I wanted to know more about what parts of the text the teacher found interesting, where I should add detail, and what kinds of details I should add. We can give our students useful feedback experiences by commenting on which components of the text work well and which ones can be improved. For example, when commenting on the piece about a ninth grader's connection between tacos and spending time with his grandparents, I identified specific attributes of the piece as well as the places in the text where those characteristics are found, such as "I was also very impressed by the way you acknowledge the history and popularity of tacos in the first paragraph" and "The second paragraph could be developed even more with this information."

I've found that identifying specific sections of students' works validates my responses and creates more of a collaborative relationship between my students and me. If my responses are vague and general, it's difficult for students to understand why I'm making the statements I am. However, if I'm noting specific attributes that work well and some that can be even stronger, it's much easier for students reading my comments to know how I've formed my evaluation of the piece. Specific statements about the piece also help me send a message to students that I want to work with them to make their writing as strong as possible. I want my students to feel that I'm coaching them through the writing process by helping them understand exactly what they're doing well and should continue, as well as what they can do to make their works even better. Concrete feedback on strengths and suggested areas of improvement can convey to students that I see the positives in their works and want to help them make their pieces even stronger.

2. Personalize the feedback that you give to each student.

Providing students with personalized feedback is another way to foster a collaborative relationship that helps students see your evaluation as intended to coach, not judge. Some particularly effective ways to provide students with personalized feedback are making connections to the content of the students' previous works, acknowledging a student's improvement and recent areas of focus, and noting similarities between the student's work and his or her interests. While the specifics of these strategies vary, they all involve knowing our students and their works well and using that knowledge in our responses to their works. In my response to the previously described essay, "#TacoTogetherness," I commented on how well the author had done using a writing strategy that he had targeted as an area of improvement; after praising his use of descriptive language, I wrote "I know you've been working on this—very nice work!" Another student in this class composed a poem about her experiences learning to use chopsticks when eating a Chinese restaurant with her stepfather. Since she had previously written about using chopsticks for her process-analysis essay (in which students explain the steps of a process), I included in my response that this poem helped me further understand the importance to her life of the topic of that previous work. The most important aspect of giving our students personalized feedback isn't the specific personal connection we make: it's showing our students that we acknowledge them as individuals and using relevant individualized information to provide them with written responses specific to them.

Final Thoughts on Responding to Student Writing in Meaningful and Useful Ways

- ◆ Meaningful and useful responses to student writing are selective, personalized responses that help students continue to feel ownership of their works.
- ◆ I've identified three ways for teachers to provide their students with these kinds of responses:
  - ◆ Select one or two piece-specific areas of growth.
  - ◆ Be sure the areas of growth are within students' abilities.
  - ◆ Use the responses to identify strengths in students' works.

◆ Meaningful responses to student writing can empower students and develop their metacognitive awareness.
   ◆ Responses to student writing that recognize what students have done well and make specific suggestions that are within students' reach can empower students by acknowledging their abilities and showing them meaningful and accessible ways to improve.
   ◆ Effective responses can increase students' metacognitive awareness of writing strategies by helping them recognize which strategies they've mastered and which ones they'll target in their future works.
◆ When putting the ideas and strategies discussed in this chapter into action, keep the following recommendations in mind, as they can increase the usefulness of the feedback you give your students:
   ◆ Identify specific sections of the text in your response.
   ◆ Personalize the feedback that you give to each student.

7

Conduct Student-Centered Writing Conferences

Now, let's explore another tactic for giving students feedback on their writing: verbal writing conferences about student work. First, we'll examine the features of writing conferences and then discuss why this strategy is important to effective English instruction. After that, we'll look inside an English classroom and check out how I recently conducted writing conferences with my ninth graders. Finally, we'll unpack key recommendations for putting this important instructional practice into action.

What Is It?

A writing conference is a one-on-one meeting between teacher and student designed to check in on the student's work and offer suggestions. These conferences are typically held while a piece of writing is in progress, providing formative assessment opportunities and facilitating close interaction between teacher and student. While there's no one way to hold a writing conference, I've found that the most effective conferences follow established procedures that provide the teacher and the students with clear understandings of how they will proceed. When I conduct a conference with a student about his or her work, I follow the procedures listed in Figure 7.1. (A reproducible version of this chart is available in Appendix A.)

These procedures are designed to be informative enough to provide teachers with a plan for how to conduct a conference, but also open-ended enough to give teachers the flexibility to adapt each conference to the needs of specific students and their works. (I've used them when conferring with students about informational pieces, argument essays,

Figure 7.1 Writing Conference Procedures

Order	Action
Step one	Ask the student to summarize the piece she or he is writing.
Step two	Ask the student to explain what she or he has done so far and what she or he plans to do.
Step three	Have the student read her or his piece out loud. While the student does this, make notes about specific strengths of the piece and ways the piece could be even stronger.
Step four	Share with the student a specific strength of the piece, citing specific evidence.
Step five	Make one suggestion for enhancing the piece by either introducing a new writing strategy or revisiting one you've previously taught. Provide the student with concrete recommendations for how this strategy could be integrated into her or his work.

short stories, poems, and literacy analyses.) No matter the genre in which the student is writing, these procedures are intended to help the teacher understand the piece the student is creating, get a sense of the writing the student has done up to that time, identify a strength the student has exhibited, and a provide a concrete suggestion designed to specifically enhance that work.

For example, I recently conferred with a middle-school student who was creating a collection of five poems about his experiences as a basketball player for his school. After he explained the project, he read to me what he had written at that time: an initial draft of the first poem in the collection. This poem, titled "Free Throws," is about the student missing a free throw in a game and then practicing free throws at home in the dark that night in front of his house. After listening to the piece, I praised the way the poem uses a lot of sensory images to show that the speaker was practicing at night, such as descriptions of "sunset," "moonlight," "streetlamps," and "hearing mosquitoes at night." Finally, I made a suggestion for improving the work even further before submitting it as a final draft: since the author does a lot of "telling" of his emotions in the poem (he states that he's "disappointed" and "determined"), I talked with him about ways to use actions to express these feelings instead.

Now that we've examined the fundamental features of a writing conference, the procedures that can make up an effective conference, and a description of a conference that followed those procedures, we'll look in our next section at key benefits that can come from holding one-on-one writing conferences with students.

Why Does It Matter?

Conducting writing conferences with students with my students has made an incredible impact on my writing instruction. When I began my career as an English teacher, I found that holding individual conferences allowed me to know my students well, understand their works, and provide my students with instruction directly related to their abilities. Without the opportunity to confer with my students individually, I would not be nearly as effective as a teacher: I simply wouldn't be able to reach my students as well as I do. Whole-class and small-group mini-lessons are important to writing instruction, but I believe individual conferences provide benefits that other instructional methods do not. There are three especially important reasons why I feel writing conferences are important to strong writing instruction: 1) they build relationships between teachers and students, 2) they provide opportunities for clarification, and 3) they help teachers differentiate instruction. We'll look at each of these benefits in detail in this section.

Conferences Build Relationships between Teachers and Students

Writing conferences provide teachers and students with opportunities to get to know each other in ways that large-group instruction does not: while I feel I get to know my students in whole-class discussions, the time when I learn the most about them is during one-on-one writing conferences. In these conferences, I learn a great deal about my students' interests, backgrounds, and personal experiences by reading their works—many of which reflect topics about which students are passionate—and asking questions about the experiences and interests behind those works. For example, when recently conferring with a student about her argument essay that her high school should offer more sports for female students, I learned much more than I previously knew about her athletic interests, including her passion for swimming and the fact that she recently participated in a prestigious triathlon. In later conversations with this student, I looked for opportunities to draw connections between the topics we were studying and her interest in and advocacy for girls' sports. In the book *Fires in the Bathroom: Advice for Teachers from High School Students* (Cushman, 2005), many students comment that they wish teachers would try to learn more information about them: their interests, areas of expertise, backgrounds, and communities. Writing conferences provide opportunities for English teachers to do this in individualized ways that are integrated into their regular instruction.

Conferences Provide Opportunities for Clarification

Writing conferences allow teachers the opportunity to talk with our students about what they're trying to achieve in a particular piece of writing and to ask clarifying questions about the work. This is important because it gives us teachers deeper understandings of the goals a student author has for a piece, which increases our abilities to provide feedback related to those goals. Think back to the conference procedures listed in Figure 7.1: the first two procedures involve students explaining the piece they're creating. (Step one asks students to summarize the work and step two calls for students to explain what they've done up to that point and what they intend to do.) Once I understand the piece a student is creating and what that student is trying to achieve, it's much easier for me to give him or her recommendations on how to enhance the work. For example, the student creating the previously described poem about practicing free throws told me that he wanted his poetry collection to show his passion for basketball. This goal informed my recommendation that he replace "telling" statements about his emotions with descriptions of actions that allow readers to infer his feelings: "It's a lot more convincing to readers if you say something like 'I danced on the court' instead of 'I was excited,'" I explained to him. "They'll be more likely to believe you're feeling something if you describe actions that show it. Plus, showing instead of telling is a lot more interesting to read and provides more clarity to your work."

Conferences Help Teachers Differentiate Instruction

Since they focus on providing students with feedback specific to their individual works and the writing skills displayed in those works, writing conferences are excellent opportunities for differentiation. Conferences allow for constantly changing instruction based on student needs that not only change from one student to another, but also change for individual students as they develop new skills throughout the school year (Shea, 2015). The feedback I provide students in writing conferences is based on their individualized needs, not a list of predetermined objectives. In other words, I don't approach the twenty writing conferences I'll hold with a class of high school students with the intention of discussing the same skill with each student: the recommendation I give each student is based on the attributes displayed in his or her work. Because writing conferences are so individualized, we teachers can use them to introduce advanced writing concepts to students who are ready to learn them and to provide reinforcement about fundamental writing strategies for students who are working on learning those.

When conferring with the student who wrote the previously described argument essay about her school expanding the athletic offerings for female students, I suggested that she revise her concluding paragraph so that it leaves readers with final thoughts to consider about the importance of gender equity: "Your current conclusion restates your main point—which is important," I told her, "but I think it can do even more. Let's talk about ways the conclusion can also leave readers with some final thoughts to consider about the significance of this topic and the important role it plays in all parts of society." In my conferences with other students about their argument essays, I addressed different areas of need specific to their works, such as the importance of including supporting details with one student and the importance of establishing a clear thesis statement with another. In every case, the feedback I provided each student was differentiated according to his or her individual writing skills.

Now that we've examined these key benefits of conducting one-on-one writing conferences with students, let's look at a description of my experiences putting this teaching tool into action in a ninth-grade English class.

What Does It Look Like in Action?

It's writing workshop time: one of my favorite parts of the English instructional period. The room is full of the energy that corresponds with focused students engaged in their work. My ninth graders are working independently on informational essays and I'm moving around the room with my writing conference binder under my arm, pulling my chair up next to individual students and holding one-on-one conferences with them. On the whiteboard in front of the room are six names, representing the students with whom I plan to confer that day. I've met with the first two students on the list and now move to the third one, a young man writing an informational piece on former United States Vice President Aaron Burr.

In this conference—like all of the conferences I conduct—I plan to follow the five-step process described earlier in this chapter in Figure 7.1; in this process, the student describes the piece and reads it to the teacher, who identifies a specific strength of the work and makes a concrete suggestion for improvement. I begin the conference by asking the student author to give me an overview of the essay.

"I'm writing my informational essay about Aaron Burr," he explains. "I've been really interested in him since I saw *Hamilton* and have been reading more about him and researching his life."

"Awesome!" I respond. "Talk to me about what you've done so far and what you'll do next."

"Well, so far I've only written the introduction," he answers. "The introduction gives some background information on Aaron Burr and sets up the rest of the essay by explaining what aspects of Burr I'm going to discuss. In the rest of the essay, I'll describe some key things about Aaron Burr that a lot of people might not know: he was a successful lawyer, an influential politician, and a supporter of women being educated."

"That all sounds really good," I tell the student. "Now, would you please read me what you've written so far?"

"Sure," he replies. The student opens a document on his laptop containing the text depicted in Figure 7.2, places the laptop between us (so that I can follow along as he reads), and reads the following text:

Figure 7.2 Student's Initial Introduction to Aaron Burr Essay

Aaron Burr: A Deeper Look

Aaron Burr was born in 1754 in Newark, New Jersey and died in 1836 in Staten Island, New York. He fought in the Revolutionary War and is best known for his role in a famous duel in which he shot and killed former Treasury Secretary Alexander Hamilton. However, there is a lot more to Aaron Burr than most people know. Burr is significant for his success as a lawyer, his impact as a politician, and his support for the education of women.

After the student reads the excerpt, I identify a strength of the work: "This introductory paragraph has a very clear thesis statement," I note. "When I read the last sentence of the paragraph, I have a great understanding of what you'll discuss in the essay."

"Thanks, I was really working on that," he comments.

"It shows," I continue. "This is a really structured introductory paragraph, but I think it could be even stronger with a more gripping hook. Instead of beginning the paragraph with information about the years in which Burr was born and died, I'd love to see that first sentence grab the reader's attention with one of the hook strategies we talked about." I point to a chart on the classroom wall that lists several tactics we discussed as a class for beginning a piece in an engaging way, such as beginning in the middle of the action, opening with dialogue, and asking a question.

"I can totally do that," asserts the student. "Maybe I can start in the middle of the action at the Burr-Hamilton duel and then explain how there's much more to what Burr did in his life than that."

"That sounds wonderful!" I exclaim. "I can't wait to see what your new introduction looks like. I'm excited to see it when we have our next conference in a few days."

Now, let's fast forward to three days later, when I next meet with this student for writing conference. He excitedly opens his laptop and shares the text depicted in Figure 7.3.

"Fantastic job!" I praise the student's work. "I love the revisions you made here: the opening is wonderfully engaging and sets up a nice transition to the idea that there's a lot more to Burr's life than many people know. You also did a really nice job of using a question in this paragraph to help the reader reflect. Also, good job keeping that strong thesis statement.

Figure 7.3 Student's Revised Introduction to Aaron Burr Essay

Aaron Burr: A Deeper Look

"Bang!" Gunshots fire in the early morning of Weehawken, New Jersey on July 11th, 1804. A bullet from Vice President Aaron Burr's pistol pierces the side of former Treasury Secretary Alexander Hamilton, eventually killing him.

When you hear the name "Aaron Burr," is this duel what you think of? For most people, it is. However, there is a lot more to Aaron Burr's life than many people know. While it's easy to just associate him with this one event, Aaron Burr's life is complex and is important to American history for many reasons. Burr is significant for his success as a lawyer, his impact as a politician, and his support for the education of women.

Now, go ahead and get started on developing the body paragraphs of the essay. I'm excited to see what you create!"

Key Tips

Now, let's examine two suggestions that can maximize the effectiveness of the writing conferences you hold with your students: 1) document the conference and 2) establish a classroom routine for holding conferences. These recommendations can ensure that your conferences are useful and organized. We'll look at these suggestions in detail by exploring what each one looks like in practice and the benefits associated with it.

1. Document the conference.

At the beginning of my first year of teaching, I held wonderful writing conferences with my students, but I quickly realized that I also needed a documentation system to make the conferences as beneficial as possible to my teaching and my students' learning. I created a documentation form that I completed during each conference I held and still use today; the form is depicted in Figure 7.4 and a reproducible version is available in Appendix A.

Once I started using this form, I had a much easier time conducting conferences and monitoring my students' progress. I fill out most of the form during the conference and take another minute afterwards to check over my notes for completion and accuracy. As I talk with the student,

Figure 7.4 Writing Conference Documentation Form

Student name and date	
Current piece	
Notes about piece	
What I most liked	
Suggestion for improvement	

I first record the title of the current piece and then make notes about the student's goals and progress. After the student reads the piece out loud (and I follow along), I record what I most liked about the piece and one suggestion for making the work even stronger. For example, in the previously described conference with the student writing about Aaron Burr, I wrote "Clear and focused thesis statement" for what I most liked and "Grab the reader's attention with one of our gripping hook strategies" as a suggestion for improvement.

One reason this documentation system is beneficial is the way it emphasizes student accountability: before I documented my conferences, I didn't have a way to monitor students' progress and remind them of the suggestions I made for enhancing their works. When I began using this form, my conferences became much easier: when I met with a student about a piece, I had a clear record of where the student was in our last meeting and what I recommended she or he do next. Because the students know I have this form and that I fill it out during every conference, they're aware that I'm monitoring their progress and the work they've done to enhance their pieces. When putting this system into action in your classes, I recommend using a binder to hold the conference forms for each class you teach. In that binder, make a section for each student indicated by binder dividers (in my experience, students love decorating their dividers!). In each section, insert several copies of the conference form and fill out a form while you conduct each conference.

2. Establish a classroom routine for holding conferences.

If you're like many teachers I know, you probably still have an important question about writing conferences: "What do I do with the other students while I'm conducting a conference?" I recommend addressing this issue by creating a routine that you'll use consistently when conducting writing conferences with students. The most important component of the routine is that students are able to work as independently as possible while you're conferring with individual students. I only hold writing conferences during the writing workshop time, an instructional period in

Figure 7.5 Guidelines for Students Who Need Help during Independent Writing

What to do if you need help during independent writing:

- ◆ First, try a reference book! Dictionaries, thesauruses, and style guides are located on the "Reference" shelf of the classroom library.
- ◆ If that doesn't work, ask someone at your table (if you feel it's a question a peer can answer).
- ◆ If you still need help, write your name on the whiteboard under the heading "Needs Help." I will come to you as soon as I can. (You can move on to another section of your piece while you wait.)

which students work independently on the works they're creating at the time. At the beginning of each writing workshop period, I write on the whiteboard the names of the students with whom I plan to confer that day. Once the independent writing time begins, I meet with the students on my list, marking through each name after I meet with the student.

To maximize the likelihood that I'll be able to conduct the conferences with little to no interruptions, I post guidelines for students to follow when they need help during independent writing—these guidelines are depicted in Figure 7.5 and available in reproducible form in Appendix A.

It often takes a few weeks at the beginning of the school year to get students accustomed to this routine, but once they are, writing conferences tend to run smoothly and without interruption. The most effective writing workshop classes prioritize independence: students' abilities to work independently on their works and teachers' opportunities to confer independently with students and provide them with individualized instruction. This classroom routine encourages independence and maximizes the effectiveness of conferences.

Final Thoughts on Conducting Student-Centered Writing Conferences

- ◆ A writing conference is a one-on-one meeting between teacher and student designed to check in on the student's work and offer suggestions.
- ◆ Conferences are typically held while a piece of writing is in progress, providing formative assessment opportunities and facilitating close interaction between teacher and student.
- ◆ There are three especially important reasons why I feel writing conferences are important to strong writing instruction: 1) they build relationships between teachers and students, 2) they provide opportunities for clarification, and 3) they help teachers differentiate instruction.

- ◆ Conferences build relationships between teachers and students by providing them with opportunities to get to know each other in ways that large-group instruction does not.
- ◆ They provide opportunities for clarification by giving teachers opportunities to talk with students about what they're trying to achieve in a particular piece of writing and to ask clarifying questions about the work.
- ◆ Conferences help teachers differentiate instruction because they focus on providing students with feedback specific to their individual works and the writing skills displayed in those works.
- ◆ When holding one-on-one writing conferences with your students, I recommend keeping the following suggestions in mind; doing so can maximize the effectiveness of your conferences:
  - ◆ Document the conference using a conference form such as the one depicted in Figure 7.4.
  - ◆ Establish a classroom routine for holding conferences; the document in Figure 7.5 provides an example of such a routine.

8

Utilize Exit Questions

For our final chapter on assessment strategies, we'll examine an effective and easy-to-use method of assessment: exit questions. We'll begin with a description of exit questions and then move to a discussion of how they are important to English instruction. After that, we'll look at how I recently used this strategy when teaching a ninth-grade English class. To conclude, we'll consider key recommendations that can help you put exit questions into action in your own classroom.

What Is It?

An exit question—also sometimes called an exit slip—is an activity done at the end of class period in which students answer a question or respond to a prompt related to the main focus of the day's lesson. When I ask my students to respond to exit questions, I ask each student to write down a response that she or he will turn in before leaving the class. Before I dismiss the class, I ask for some students to share their responses out loud. For example, at the end of a class in which I talked with a group of sixth graders about how writers use prepositional phrases, I posed the question, "How can prepositional phrases improve a piece of writing?" as the day's exit question. I presented the question with five minutes left in the class period and gave them two minutes to write a response to the day's question. After they took this time to write down their thoughts, I asked for volunteers to verbally share their insights with the rest of the class. Once a few students shared, I instructed all of the students to leave their written exit question responses on a table at the front of the room.

I feel the most essential attribute of a strong exit question is that it asks students to reflect on the lesson's topic and synthesize the information they've learned. I always caution new teachers to avoid exit questions that focus only on specific facts, as these responses will not provide students with meaningful reflection opportunities and the chance to synthesize important information. For example, an effective exit question for a class period focused on the first chapter of *The Great Gatsby* could be, "What is an inference you can draw about one of the characters we meet in this chapter?" while an ineffective one would be "What sport did Nick Buchanan play in college?" The first question asks students to reflect on information discussed in the day's class and draw conclusions based on it, while the second asks for a detail from the text. As a teacher, I would find students' responses to the first question to be useful data for formative assessment, as the answers would convey what they're noticing about the characters in the novel up to this point and the related inferences they're making. In contrast, the answers to the second question wouldn't tell me anything about students' thoughts or insights; it would just let me know if they recall a piece of information.

The chart depicted in Figure 8.1 describes key components of exit questions.

Now that we've explored the fundamental components of exit questions, let's consider why they're important to effective English instruction.

Figure 8.1 Key Components of Exit Questions

Components	Explanations
What is an exit question?	An exit question is an activity done at the end of class period in which students answer a question or respond to a prompt related to the main focus of the day's lesson.
What should exit questions do?	Exit questions should ask students to reflect on the lesson's topic and synthesize the information they've learned.
What should exit questions avoid?	When creating exit questions, teachers should avoid asking questions that focus only on specific facts, as these kinds of questions don't allow for reflection and synthesis.
What are some examples of exit questions?	"How can prepositional phrases improve a piece of writing?" "What is an inference you can draw about one of the characters we meet in the first chapter of *The Great Gatsby?*"

Why Does It Matter?

A class period without an exit question would still perform its fundamental purpose, but wouldn't be as beneficial to students as it could be. By using exit questions, we teachers can help our students take the maximum benefit from their instructional time. In this section, we'll explore three key benefits that come from the use of exit questions: 1) exit questions facilitate reflective thinking, 2) they give teachers daily assessment information, and 3) they allow students to learn from one another. Let's examine each of these benefits individually.

Exit Questions Facilitate Reflective Thinking

Students who respond to exit questions about key concepts can grow as reflective learners: by performing the tasks exit questions require (such as synthesizing important information and considering the importance of a topic), students develop the ability to think in thoughtful and metacognitive ways. Whenever I teach my students about a writing or reading strategy, I ask in the exit question why that strategy is important. Recall the example from earlier in this chapter in which I asked sixth graders why prepositional phrases are important to effective writing; the students' responses to this question showed that they were thoughtfully reflecting on the significance of this concept. One student shared that "Prepositional phrases are important because of all the detail they add. Without them, you might not know where or when something happened, like 'in the classroom' or 'after lunch.'" Another asserted that "Without prepositional phrases, sentences would just be really basic. They wouldn't have much to them except for basic information." These responses showed me that the students were thoughtfully reflecting on the importance of the concept we discussed that day, which was my goal for the exit question.

Exit Questions Give Teachers Daily Assessment Information

An important challenge for teachers of all experience levels is acquiring regular assessment data on students to monitor their progress and determine what supports they need—waiting to see students' performances on large-scale papers and projects is often not enough. Formative assessments such as exit questions give teachers low-stakes insights in how well their students are understanding important material, while summative assessments at the end of a project or unit typically have grades attached to them are administered in higher-pressure situations. When I was a new teacher, I thought I'd be able to evaluate my students daily based on only their comments in class discussions; while the students' comments provided some material for formative assessment, it wasn't enough for me to form meaningful conclusions about what supports and scaffolds individual students needed. Exit questions solved this problem by providing me with daily information about how well students were understanding key concepts; as I read through the day's exit question responses after school, I noted any confusion or misunderstandings the students' responses conveyed, as well as information that students appeared to understand quite well.

For example, I once asked a seventh-grade English class to answer the exit question "Why is sensory imagery an important tool for effective writing?" The students' responses gave me insight into how well they understood sensory imagery and its significance. Most students' answers showed strong understandings of this concept and its importance, although one student's response suggested that he was confused about the definition of sensory imagery and why it can be an attribute of effective writing. During the next class, I met with him individually about this topic, reviewing what sensory imagery is and further explaining the importance of this concept to strong writing to help him understand. The students' exit question responses showed me what they knew and who needed additional support, helping me be an aware and effective teacher.

Exit Questions Allow Students to Learn From One Another

Asking students to share their exit question responses verbally creates an opportunity for individuals to learn from their classmates' insights and ideas. To bring this benefit to fruition, I like to have two or three students share their exit responses verbally after they've written down their answers. While I generally do this by asking for volunteers, I'll vary this practice by calling on students if I notice that some students are dominating the sharing time and/or others are not sharing their insights. Whether the comments come from volunteers or from people who are called on, students who hear their peers' responses can compare their thoughts with those that their classmates share. For example, after discussing Virginia Woolf's novel *Mrs. Dalloway* with a group of high school seniors, I gave the students an exit question asking them to identify the character with whom they felt the strongest personal connection and why. The students not only enjoyed hearing which characters their classmates compared themselves to, but also deepened their understandings of the novel and its characters by listening to their peers' insights. Similarly, when I asked seventh-graders to comment on the importance of sensory imagery to effective writing, they responded in a variety of ways that enhanced the understandings of other students in the class. One student explained that sensory details are important because they call attention to really important information, while another explained that sensory imagery helps readers feel like they're in the middle of the action. While these responses have similarities, they also are distinct enough that students can learn new insights and approaches by listening to both assertions.

As these explanations and examples indicate, exit questions can be beneficial to both teachers and students by providing regular assessment data, fostering reflective thinking, and giving students opportunities to learn from their peers. In the next section, we'll take a look inside a ninth-grade English class and examine how I use exit questions with those students.

What Does It Look Like in Action?

Prior to today, my ninth graders seemed to have strong understandings of every component of argument writing, except for one: writing effective conclusions. Many of my students' conclusions were brief summaries of their argument essays, so I used today's class to help them write conclusions that are more informative and thought-provoking. We discussed how strong conclusions to argument essays are more than simple summaries: they are carefully constructed sections that emphasize the significance of the cause for which the essay is arguing and leave readers with a final thought about the piece's claim (Ruday, 2016). Early in the class period, I introduced these ideas, explaining what they look like in practice and why they're important to effective argument writing. Then, we looked together at examples of strong conclusions that contain these components and discussed how these features made the examples stronger than if they only summarized previously discussed information.

Now, we're at the end of the class period, which means it's time for the exit question. I project the image in Figure 8.2, a slide containing the day's exit question, to the front of the room.

Figure 8.2 Exit Question Example

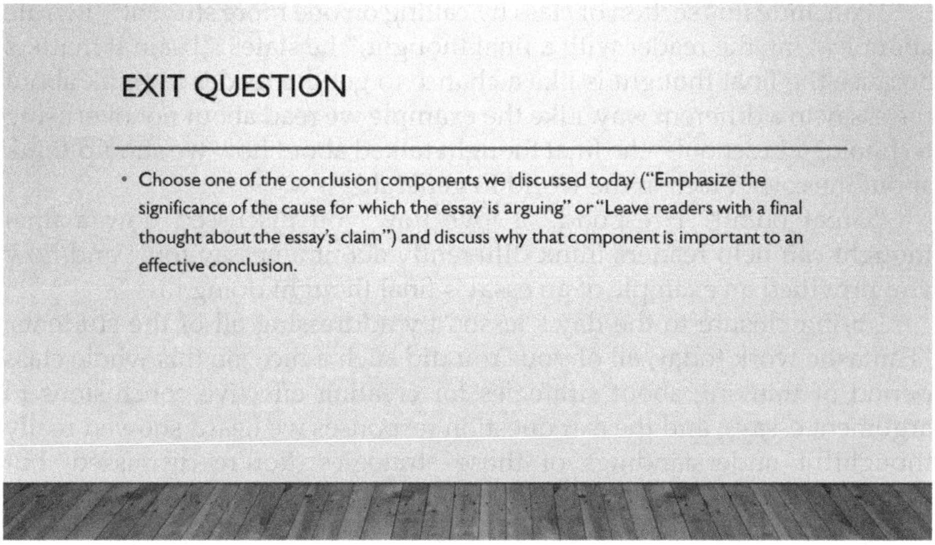

EXIT QUESTION

• Choose one of the conclusion components we discussed today ("Emphasize the significance of the cause for which the essay is arguing" or "Leave readers with a final thought about the essay's claim") and discuss why that component is important to an effective conclusion.

When I discuss multiple strategies during a class period (as was the case in this lesson with the two conclusion components we considered), I'll often ask the students to select one of the strategies we discussed to reflect on when completing the exit question. This keeps the exit questions relatively brief—keeping them consistent with their purpose as a short formative assessment—and gives students a bit of flexibility in their responses; this flexibility is especially valuable when students share their responses out loud, as it increases the likelihood that students will learn new ideas and insights from listening to their peers.

The students take about two minutes to write their answers to the exit question before I ask for three volunteers to share their responses. I call on the first student to raise a hand; she explains, "I wrote about how it's important to leave readers with a final thought. I said doing that is really important to writing a good conclusion because the final thought is what stays with the reader. If you didn't leave a final thought, your essay wouldn't be memorable, which means it would be as good."

"Wonderful response!" I exclaim. "You did a great job of describing the benefits of leaving readers with a final thought about a topic; I thought your statement about the importance of an essay being memorable to the reader was particularly insightful."

Next, I call on a student who shares, "I picked the one about emphasizing the significance of the cause you're arguing for. I think doing that's important because, like you said earlier in class, you want to make sure readers understand that they just read about something that matters."

"Really nicely said," I reply. "You're right: you want your reader to finish the essay and think, 'I just read about a significant topic.' You don't want the reader to think, 'Why did I just bother reading that?' Emphasizing the significance of the cause helps the reader understand its importance."

I conclude this section of class by calling on one more student: "I wrote about leaving the reader with a final thought," he states. "I said it matters because the final thought is like a chance to get the reader to think about the essay in a different way. Like the example we read about not overusing technology in school—the final thought talked about how we should think about the role of tech in the world in general."

"Great point!" I respond. "I love how you discussed how a final thought can help readers think differently about an essay topic and how you provided an example of an essay's final thought doing this."

I bring closure to the day's lesson by addressing all of the students: "Fantastic work today, all of you. You did such a nice job this whole class period of thinking about strategies for creating effective conclusions to argument essays, and the exit question responses we heard showed really thoughtful understandings of those strategies. You're dismissed, but before you head out, please leave your exit question responses on the table in the front of the room. Great job today!"

Key Tips

Now, let's examine two recommendations that can make your implementation of exit questions as effective as possible: 1) align exit questions with key instructional goals and 2) consider the many ways exit questions can inform instruction. These suggestions can help you create meaningful exit questions and use students' responses to those questions to provide them with support that's relevant to their levels of understanding. Let's explore what each one of these suggestions means and the benefits associated with it.

1. Align exit questions with key instructional goals.

When I talk with new teachers about the use of exit questions, I emphasize the importance of crafting effective questions: "Exit questions can be outstanding instructional strategies," I recently explained in a professional development workshop, "but they're really only useful if you ask the right questions: questions that align with your main instructional goal for the day." To generate strong exit questions, I recommend asking yourself, "What do I want my students to understand as a result of today's lesson?" Your answer to this question can then form the basis for a meaningful exit question. For example, in the lesson described in the preceding section, I asked the students an exit question that aligned with the conclusion attributes that I wanted them to understand and be able to use in their writing. By asking students why one of the strategies we discussed is important to crafting a strong conclusion, I ensured that the students' responses to the exit questions would provide me with useful information. Since my question aligned with the major instructional objective of the day, the students' answers let me know how well they grasped the focal component of the lesson.

2. Consider the many ways exit questions can inform instruction.

Once you've crafted an exit question that aligns with your key instructional objective for a lesson, you can consider how the students' responses to that question can impact your instruction. There are a number of ways you can use the results of exit questions to provide your students with needed support: small group mini-lessons, individual check-ins, and whole-class review mini-lessons are all useful tactics. To determine which one to use, consider what needs the students' exit question responses suggest they have and the number of students whose comments reveal those needs. In the case of several students needing some extra support or explanation, I'll hold a small-group mini-lesson with those students, asking them to meet briefly with me during the day's independent work time. If only one student needs the extra support, I'll meet with that person individually. If at least half of the class shows some confusion, I'll review the topic as part of a whole-class mini-lesson.

For example, after I asked my ninth graders to complete the exit question about the conclusion components we discussed, I reviewed their responses to check their levels of understanding. While most of the students understood the topic very well, there were two individuals who seemed to need some extra help understanding the idea of leaving the reader with a final thought about the essay's claim. Both of their exit responses suggested that they thought leaving the reader with a final thought meant summarizing the thesis statement, while my goal was for students to see this as a chance to allow readers to reflect on a key idea that is both related to the essay's topic and relevant to broader social issues, such as the impact of technology or the goal of education. When I met with the two students who seemed to need some extra support, I further described the idea of leaving readers with a final thought about an argument essay's claim, reviewing the examples we looked at in class the previous day and showing them some new ones to further reinforce the concept. This follow-up discussion, which took place because of the students' responses to their exit questions, significantly improved the students' understandings of this topic.

Final Thoughts on Utilizing Exit Questions

- ◆ An exit question is an activity done at the end of class period in which students answer a question or respond to a prompt related to the main focus of the day's lesson.
- ◆ Exit questions should ask students to reflect on the lesson's topic and synthesize the information they've learned (and avoid addressing only specific facts about the material).
- ◆ There are three especially important benefits I associate with the use of exit questions: 1) exit questions facilitate reflective thinking, 2) they give teachers daily assessment information, and 3) they allow students to learn from one another.
  - ◆ Exit questions facilitate reflective thinking because they require students to synthesize important information and consider a topic's significance—tasks that develop students' abilities to respond in thoughtful and metacognitive ways.
  - ◆ They give teachers daily assessment information by providing regular data that conveys how well students are understanding key concepts.
  - ◆ Exit questions allow students to learn from one another because they create opportunities for students to share their

reflections verbally, allowing students to hear their class-mates' insights and learn from their perspectives.

◆ When putting exit questions into action in your classroom, I recommend following two key recommendations to maximize their instructional benefits:

- ◆ Align exit questions with key instructional goals.
- ◆ Consider the many ways exit questions can inform instruction.

Section **3**

Work-Life Balance Strategies

9

Communicate Actively and Carefully with Students and Families

In this chapter, we'll begin our exploration of work-life balance strategies for new English teachers by considering the idea of communicating effectively with students and their families. First, we'll examine what it means for educators to communicate actively and carefully and then consider why doing this is so important to being successful as a new teacher. After that, we'll look at an example of what this strategy can look like in practice before concluding with some final recommendations to keep in mind when communicating with your students and their families.

What Is It?

The strategy of communicating actively and carefully with your students and their families can be summarized as being as proactive as possible in your communication to ensure that your instructions, policies, and choices are being understood in the manner in which you intend. The more you communicate with students and families, the more opportunities you'll have to make sure they understand what you want them to know. In this section, we'll explore three key tactics for communicating clearly and effectively with students and families: weekly or biweekly family newsletters, weekly student agendas, and classroom websites. Let's examine each of these communication methods individually.

Family Newsletters

Creating a weekly or biweekly newsletter that you share with your students' families is a great tactic for fostering an environment of active communication. I send these newsletters home on Fridays via email and use them to discuss key topics that we've covered that week, as well as upcoming assignments and events. Figure 9.1 contains an example of a weekly newsletter that I've used when communicating with my ninth graders' families. It summarizes our work the past week and provides information about upcoming assignments; I use the same template each week, replacing the old material and filling in the new and relevant information. I encourage you to find a regular structure to use with your students; it will save you time (compared to using a different structure each time) and provide families information in a predictable way.

Figure 9.1 Family Newsletter Example

English 9 Honors Family Newsletter
October 13th, 2017

What We've Been Up To

Reading

On Monday, we began our "More than Meets the Eye!" reading workshop project, which focuses on how characters in texts often have attributes and qualities for which others don't initially give them credit. For this project, we're using the novel *Bronx Masquerade* by Nikki Grimes as a whole-class read aloud. We've been discussing how the characters in that book are perceived in certain ways and how those perceptions often don't align with their nuanced, complex interests and personalities. Students are looking for similar themes in their independent reading books and will record their observations and insights in their reading response journals.

Writing

In writing, we're making great progress with our "Object History" research project, in which students select a type of object and research its history, including its origin, major ways it has developed, and the reasons behind its significant changes.

Language Study

We're continuing to study Greek and Latin roots in language study; scores from Wednesday's quiz have been entered on Blackboard.

What's Coming Up

Reading

We're continuing with the "More than Meets the Eye!" project. Students should read their independent reading texts for 20 minutes a night and note "More than Meets the Eye!" connections in their reading response journals.

Writing

On Friday, October 20th, the final drafts of our "Object History" pieces are due. Students will be instructed to bring a hard copy of their piece to class that day. We'll also have the publishing celebration for those works on October 20th in first period. As always, families are invited to take part in the festivities and hear students read excerpts from their works. Students have received hard copies of the rubric for this assignment; electronic copies of the rubric are available on the class website.

Language Study

Our next Greek and Latin roots quiz is on Wednesday, October 18th. Students have received copies of the roots for the quiz; these roots are also available on the class website.

As always, just let me know if you have any questions or would like to discuss anything!

Weekly Student Agendas

Just as family newsletters create an environment of active communication with families, weekly student agendas foster a feeling of communication with students. Agendas are outlines of the material covered for the week and the homework and assignments relevant to each day. I like to give my students these agendas at the beginning of class each Monday so they understand what we'll be exploring that week. These agendas tend to provide students with a sense of focus, as they send the message that there is important academic work to be done that will take the students' best efforts. In addition, they're useful for letting students know what work they missed when absent—once I started distributing weekly agendas to my students, I no longer had to worry about students saying they didn't know what the homework was when they missed class.

Figure 9.2 contains an excerpt from a student agenda I recently used with a ninth-grade English class; it lists reading, writing, and language study work planned for the first two days of that week.

When constructing agendas for your classes, I recommend dividing each day by topic, like this one does: separating each class into its components helps students understand the different material we'll cover and gives them a sense of how each day's class will be structured, providing them with clear expectations for each day's material and procedures.

Classroom Websites

Classroom websites are excellent tools for facilitating communication with students and families. I use my classroom website as a repository for key information that my students and their families can access whenever they need to. On the website, I archive the family newsletters and student agendas I create throughout the school year, as well other important documents such as rubrics for major assignments and lists of the word roots we use for language study. I explain to the students and families at the beginning of the school year that the family newsletters and student agendas are my main method of communication and that the website is a "storage unit" of sorts where they can always go when they need to access one of the documents housed there. I highly recommend making a class website to store key documents: it will save you a great deal of time by eliminating emails from students who misplaced their rubrics, agendas, or vocabulary lists.

Figure 9.3 depicts a screen shot of the home page classroom website I'm currently using with my students; each tab near the top of the page identifies where to go for specific types of materials. If you use a website with your classes, I recommend introducing it at the beginning of the school year: on the first day of classes with your students and in the first newsletter you send home to the students' families (with a hands-on tutorial at back-to-school night). By describing the site and its functionality as

Figure 9.2 Weekly Agenda Excerpt

English 9 Honors Agenda: Week of October 15th–20th, 2017

Monday, October 15th

Reading

Read aloud: *Bronx Masquerade*

Independent reading

Response journal: Compare a character in your book with a character in *Bronx Masquerade*

Writing

Mini-lesson: Transition statements

Independent writing: Focus on transition statements in your "Object History" pieces

Share time: Share a transition statement

Homework

Read your independent reading book for 20 minutes; respond to one of our sample prompts in your response journal

Tuesday, October 16th

Language Study

Review for Wednesday's Greek and Latin root quiz

Reading

Read aloud: *Bronx Masquerade*

Independent reading

Response journal: What is an important relationship to the protagonist of your independent reading book?

Writing

Mini-lesson: Semicolon use

Independent writing: Keep working on object history pieces, keeping semicolon use in mind

Share time: Did you incorporate semicolons in your piece? Why or why not?

Homework

Read your independent reading book for 20 minutes; respond to one of our sample prompts in your response journal

Study for Greek and Latin root quiz on Wednesday

Figure 9.3 Classroom Website Example

ENGLISH NINE HONORS WITH DR. RUDAY

HOME   NEWSLETTERS   AGENDAS   RUBRICS   LANGUAGE STUDY

Note: There is a wide range of possible site platforms. The site depicted in Figure 9.3 was made with a template on weebly.com, but many possibilities exist and some schools will allow you to make a page on the school-specific site. I suggest trying out a few options and seeing what support your school can provide.

early as possible, you'll maximize the likelihood that your students their families will take advantage of its usefulness.

Why Does It Matter?

Now that we've examined some examples of active communication with students and families, let's consider why this practice is important to the success of a new English teacher. By using the tactics described in the preceding section to communicate in active and careful ways with your students and their families, you'll achieve three key benefits, each described in detail in this section: 1) keep students on track for success, 2) create partnerships with families, and 3) facilitate the flow of your instruction. A common thread among these benefits is the idea that effective communication is proactive instead of reactive. I advise new teachers to share important information with students and families as early as possible to avoid confusion. By taking an active role in communicating by sharing detailed information in a regular format, you'll help students and families feel informed and empowered, reducing potential stressors and allowing more time in the classroom to be devoted to teaching and learning.

Keep Students on Track for Success

Continued active communication through weekly agendas provides students with the information they need to stay on track in your classes. By letting students know what assignments are due and what material will be covered each week (and making that information available online through a repository such as a class website), you'll create a supportive environment that shows students you want them to be successful. One of my beliefs about effective teaching—and one that I work to put into practice with all students I teach—is that teachers should set high expectations for their students and give them the necessary support to reach those expectations; giving students clear understandings of the assignments they have coming due, as well as the rubrics and study guides they need to do well on these assignments, facilitates both academic rigor and an environment of support. I recently asked the ninth-grade students I've been working with to complete an assessment of my instruction and several of them commented on the support they felt they received through frequent communication; one asserted "We learn a lot, but it doesn't feel crazy stressful or anything because you always let us know what's going on and where we can get things like rubrics and agendas if we need them. That's really helpful!"

Create Partnerships With Families

By sending home newsletters that inform students' families of the material students are learning in your class, upcoming assignments, and opportunities for involvement, you're doing more than just sharing information: you're building relationships with people who can become your strongest advocates. I've found that informing families of the goings-on in my classes has communicated to them that I really care about working with them to help their student succeed. I witnessed firsthand the impact of forming family partnerships during my first year of teaching: during a parent-teacher conference, a student's mother told me that she knows I "really care" about her daughter's success because of "all the time it must take" to send home family newsletters and student agendas. She explained to me, "I always tell [my daughter] to work hard for your class because I know you really care." This conversation was eye-opening to me because it conveyed the importance this parent attached to my communication with students and families: not only did she note the time it took, but also the idea that I would only do this if I was invested in the students' successes. Active communication is a great way to send the message that we want our students to succeed.

Facilitate the Flow of Your Instruction

Another key benefit of active communication is that it helps you devote your instructional time to teaching and learning instead of using that time to remind students of assignments and deadlines. Once I started providing students with agendas and families with newsletters (and posting these documents and other resources on the class website), I was struck by how little time I needed to spend in class making sure students were aware of upcoming assignments. Other than the five or so minutes I spend with my students each Monday morning giving them the week's agenda and going over it with them, I'm able to spend my entire instructional time focusing on helping my students learn key material. When I talk with new and preservice teachers, I emphasize the impact that proactive communication can have on effective instruction: "If you're spending a great deal of time every day reminding students of assignments and telling them what homework is due the next day," I recently explained, "you're actually taking instructional time away from your students and from you as a teacher. It takes time on the front end to do make agendas and newsletters and post them online, but you'll be really thankful that you did when you're spending more time teaching."

While the three benefits described in this section are distinct in some ways, they also have key commonalities: all three of them are based on the idea that clear and effective communication facilitates organization, which contributes to effective learning. By communicating proactively with your students and their families, you'll help build a positive experience for your students, their families, and your instruction. In the next section, we'll take a look inside a ninth-grade class and see how I use student agendas to build an environment of clear expectations and strong communication.

What Does It Look Like in Action?

It's a sunny, crisp Monday morning in October; my students enter the classroom and find a familiar object next to the entrance: copies of the week's agenda, which I've placed on a table in the front of the room for students to pick up before heading to their seats. (This agenda is the same one excerpted in Figure 9.2.) Once the students have their agendas in hand and are at their desks, I get started: "Hey everyone! Hope your weekends were excellent. Great job picking up those agendas on your way in. Let's talk about what's going on this week."

I project the first page of the agenda to the front of the room and begin to read it out loud while the students follow along on their individual copies. "As you can see, there's a lot going on this week. A few highlights: in reading, we're continuing to work on our 'More than Meets the Eye' project, where we use *Bronx Masquerade* and our independent reading books to look at the contrasts between individuals' inner characters and how they are perceived by others. In language study, we'll have our usual Wednesday quiz; in writing, we have our final drafts of our object history pieces due on Friday and our publishing celebration that day as well. You all would get bored really quickly if I read every word of this agenda to you, and that would also take up our work time, but I wanted to be sure to give you a heads up about the important information I just mentioned.

We'll get into more of the specific reading and writing focal points on each day, like the writing strategies I'm going to ask you to incorporate into the object history piece and the themes and ideas I'll ask you to consider in your independent reading book. Put this agenda in your English folder so that you'll always be able to look at it and see what we're doing in class. Remember that there's somewhere else you can find the agenda if you lose it—this is also the same place you can also go for copies of rubrics and language study guides. It is . . ."

"The website!" a chorus of students replies.

"Very good," I smile. "The agendas are all on our class website, as are the rubrics, the guides for language study, and the family newsletters. Now, let's get started on today's work with our *Bronx Masquerade* read aloud."

Key Tips

In this section, we'll examine two recommendations that can help you put the communication strategies described in this chapter into action: 1) start using these tactics at the beginning of the school year and 2) adapt your communication material if necessary. These suggestions will help you maximize the effectiveness of the family newsletters, student agendas, and classroom website described in this chapter; let's look closely at what each recommendation means and why it can be beneficial.

1. Start using these tactics at the beginning of the school year.

To maximize the effectiveness of your communication with students and their families, I strongly recommend setting up your newsletters, agendas, and webpage before the school year starts. During the week prior to the first day of classes, I set up the website I'll use for my classes, create my first agenda and newsletter, and post these documents to the website so that students and families can access this material as soon as school starts. Then, on the first day of school, I familiarize students with these resources and send a message home to families to inform them as well.

While it can be tempting to delay this work a bit since the beginning of the school year is so busy, doing so can reduce the effectiveness of your communication: a key benefit of implementing these communication procedures at the opening of the school year is that it establishes a culture of open and frequent communication between the teacher and the students and families. The procedures and routines you establish at the beginning of the school year form the expectations and guidelines that will shape your classroom culture (Wong & Wong, 2009); beginning the year with active communication helps students and families see you as someone interest in sharing information that facilitates the students' academic successes. If y.ou institute newsletters and agendas later in the school year, the social and academic culture in your classroom might already form before you send home these materials, potentially making your communication less of a part of the classroom culture than if you instituted it at the beginning.

2. Adapt your communication material if necessary.

While I strongly recommend using newsletters, agendas, and a class website at the very beginning of the school year and continuing to do so as the year progresses, I feel that it's important for us teachers to adapt our communication material to meet our students' and families' needs. Rather than recommending a specific change, this suggestion addresses a conceptual approach to communicating with students and their families: your communication will be at its strongest if you're open to concerns students and families raise and make adjustments accordingly. For example, I was once working with a sixth-grade English class when I learned from some parents that they found the family newsletters I was sending home hard to understand—they had a hard time determining when assignments were due. (At the time, my newsletters were only separated into reading, writing, and language study; they didn't include the "What We've Been Up To" and "What's Coming Up" sections that my newsletters currently do.) I restructured the newsletters so they were organized into these two columns, with reading, writing, and language study addressed in each column. This changed worked so well that I still use it today—like the example depicted in Figure 9.1.

Another time I adapted my communication after the beginning of the school year related to the tabs I created on the classroom website: several years ago, I created a class website that contained the tabs "Newsletters," "Agendas," and "Resources" on the top of the page. Under the "Resources" tab, I uploaded the rubrics I had created for the students' written projects and the lists of words and word roots used for language study work. About two months into the school year, some students told me that, while they found the website useful, it was taking them a long time to sift through the rubrics and word lists under the "Resources" tab. To address this issue, I separated these resources into two tabs: "Rubrics" and "Language Study." Like the newsletter change described in the preceding paragraph, I continue to use this new version in my instruction today.

Final Thoughts on Communicating Actively and Carefully with Students and Families

◆ Communicating actively and carefully with your students and their families involves being as proactive as possible in your communication to ensure that your instructions, policies, and choices are being understood in the manner in which you intend.

- Three key tactics for communicating clearly and effectively with students and families are family newsletters, weekly student agendas, and classroom websites.
  - Family newsletters are documents sent home to students' families that discuss key topics the class has recently covered, as well as upcoming assignments and events.
  - Weekly student agendas are outlines of the material covered for the week and the homework and assignments relevant to each day. I like to give my students these agendas at the beginning of class each Monday so they understand what we'll be exploring that week.
  - The classroom website functions as a repository for key information that students and their families can access whenever they need to.
- Active and careful communication with students and families can keep students on track for success, create partnerships with families, and facilitate the flow of your instruction.
  - Communication keeps students on track for success by letting them know what assignments are due and what material will be covered each week, thereby creating a supportive environment that shows students you want them to be successful.
  - It creates partnerships with families by sending the message that you really care about working with them to help their students succeed.
  - It facilitates the flow of your instruction by allowing you to spend more of your instructional time on teaching and learning and less of it on reminding students of assignments and deadlines.
- When communicating with your students and their families, I recommend keeping the following suggestions in mind; they will help you maximize the effectiveness of the family newsletters, student agendas, and classroom website described in this chapter:
  - Start using these tactics at the beginning of the school year.
  - Adapt your communication material if necessary.

10

Work Effectively with Mentors

A key component of getting your career as an English teacher off to a strong start is working effectively with a mentor or network of mentors that supports and guides you (Portner, 2008). In this chapter, we'll explore the forms mentoring can take and then discuss why having a strong mentor or mentorship network is so important to the success of new English teachers. After that, we'll look at an example of what mentoring can look like in practice; finally, we'll examine some key recommendations to help you work effectively with mentors.

What Is It?

A new teacher's mentor can play a number of roles depending on the needs of the mentee and the attributes of the mentor. On the most fundamental level, a mentor provides her or his mentee with support that helps the mentee be a successful teacher. However, the specific supports the mentor provides will vary based on the needs of the mentee and the role of the mentor. In this section, we'll look at three possible kinds of mentors you might encounter as a new teacher and their similarities and differences: assigned mentors, naturally developing mentors, and online mentoring communities.

Assigned Mentors

Many schools and districts partner new teachers with experienced mentor teachers that are responsible for introducing their mentees to the school culture and serving as a resource for questions and concerns the mentees have. The mentors typically teach at the same school as the mentee, but some school districts have specially assigned mentor teachers that have mentees in several area schools. Assigned mentors will typically meet with their mentees periodically throughout the school year to answer instructional questions they have and update them on important procedures—such as the report card system, how parent-conference night is structured, and other information best learned from someone who has experienced it. Many assigned mentors will also observe their mentees' classes periodically and talk after the observation about what went well and some strategies for improvement. Since mentors are not typically evaluators, these observations are not meant to formally document the effectiveness of the mentee's instruction, but rather to provide feedback and suggestions.

Naturally Developing Mentors

While assigned mentors are excellent resources, it's likely that not every mentor you'll have will be one that's assigned to you. Many mentoring relationships develop naturally as you get to know other teachers in your school and notice attributes they have that you'd like to emulate. These relationships can develop in a variety of ways: since they aren't as formal as the relationships between assigned mentors and their mentees, they won't follow the same kind of established format. To facilitate naturally developing mentor/mentee relationships with your colleagues, I recommend being open to learning from the other teachers around you and using this openness to create a network of mentors. For example, you might get to know one teacher who has excellent classroom management techniques, another who conducts engaging mini-lessons, and another who creates imaginative assignments: try to learn from all of these individuals by asking them what works for them and then reflecting on ways you might incorporate or adapt their ideas to enhance your own instruction.

Online Mentoring Communities

Technological innovations have expanded new teachers' options for finding mentors and mentorship networks: there are many online opportunities for teachers who want to ask questions, reflect on important topics, and stay up to date on relevant issues. Like all technology-based information, online opportunities for teachers to communicate are frequently changing and developing; however, I'd like to note some especially popular and high-quality ways for new teachers to network and possibly build mentoring relationships. The National Council of Teachers of English (NCTE) has an online "Connected Community" message board (https://ncte.connectedcommunity.org/home) where teachers of all experience and interest levels can pose questions, troubleshoot problems, and explore issues together. It's common to see new teachers asking for advice on this online resource and for a diverse array of teachers to provide thoughtful responses to these questions.

Another useful resource for new teachers interested in connecting with and learning from others is Twitter: I recommend that new teachers create professional Twitter accounts that they use to connect with teachers and professional organizations and to participate in Twitter chats about educational topics. Many professional organizations that focus on teaching English and literacy—such as NCTE and the International Literacy Association (ILA), as well as regional affiliate groups of these organizations—host regular Twitter chats where moderators pose questions and participants respond to those questions and to one another's responses. I've taken part in these chats and found that participants provided thoughtful and supportive responses to statements made by teachers of all experience levels, including those new to the profession. In addition, you can continue the conversation outside of the time frame of the chat by following people with whom you'd like to remain in contact; doing this will further help you form a strong mentorship network.

All of the mentor types described in this section can form the basis of one's Professional Learning Network (PLN), "a vibrant, ever-changing group of connections to which teachers go to both share and learn" (Crowley, 2014). The individuals in a teacher's PLN often consist of the teacher's close colleagues and other teachers with whom she or he has corresponded, either in person or online. Building a support system of other teachers to whom you can turn with questions and for support is a great way to facilitate your success as a new English teacher.

Why Does It Matter?

Because of the challenges inherent in being a new teacher, schools around the world are identifying mentoring as an important need and working to provide extra support for their first-year teachers (Kent, Green, & Feldman, 2012). In this section, we'll look closely at three ways mentoring can improve the experiences and effectiveness of new teachers, examining how mentors can: 1) help teachers feel part of a community, 2) provide instructional ideas, and 3) offer guidance with managing time. Let's explore each of these ideas in detail.

Mentors Can Help New Teachers Feel Part of a Community

Due to the nature of our jobs, we teachers are frequently isolated from other adults when we're working: we are usually in our own classrooms with our students and therefore spending most of the day away from our colleagues. This feeling of isolation is often especially pronounced for new teachers, who can easily feel overwhelmed by adjusting to a school's culture, planning lessons, grading, and dealing with student issues (Kent, Green, & Feldman, 2012). One key benefit of mentoring is that new teachers can talk with others who have already experienced the same challenges. Even if you feel embarrassed at first, talk with one or more of your mentors about your frustrations and your successes: it's very likely that your mentors will have had many similar experiences. As you and your mentors talk, you'll build relationships and establish feelings of community and camaraderie. These feelings were crucial to my success as a first-year teacher: as I shared my challenges and achievements with my mentors, I felt more connected to the school community. Even on days I didn't see my mentors, the feeling that there were supportive individuals who wanted me to succeed and cared about my well-being gave me the support I needed.

Mentors Can Provide New Teachers With Instructional Ideas

In addition to helping you feel connected with other educators, mentors can provide instructional ideas and suggestions. To make the most of this benefit, I recommend identifying specific instructional goals and asking your mentor or mentors if they have any resources for helping students achieve those goals. When I've mentored new teachers, I found myself better able to provide specific resources and ideas when a mentee came to me with a concrete question such as "How can I help my students write strong introductions?" or "How do you manage the classroom during reading and writing workshop?" These specific questions allow the mentor to identify the exact need the mentee has and provide relevant resources and ideas.

When asking for instructional suggestions, I recommend making use of your entire mentorship network: ask your primary mentor for her or his input, but also present the issue to other teachers you know and elicit their feedback. In addition, it's a good idea to ask for input from teachers you interact with online, such as those in an online community where teachers ask questions and others share responses, or those that participate in teacher-focused Twitter chats. Once you receive feedback from all of these individuals, you can then examine their responses and determine which ones you'd most like to incorporate into your instruction based on how they fit with your instructional philosophy and how you see your students responding to the ideas. When I was a new teacher, I didn't implement every instructional suggestion a mentor gave me, but I did consider each one carefully and then made an educated decision about whether the recommendation would fit well with my students and my instructional philosophy.

Mentors Can Help New Teachers Manage Time

One of the most significant challenges new teachers face is managing the many demands on their time: in addition to the time they spend teaching, teachers must create lesson plans, grade, complete paperwork, organize their classrooms, communicate with parents, and other necessary tasks (Fry, 2007). While these are issues faced by all teachers, they're especially relevant to the experiences of new teachers who haven't yet developed a full arsenal of lesson plans, rubrics, and organizational systems they can adapt from year to year (Fry, 2007). Also, new English teachers have even more of a time shortage than many other subject teachers because of how long it takes to grade student work for their subject areas (Jago, 2005). Given all of these challenges, it's important for new English teachers to rely on their mentors to help them devise some time-management strategies.

I encourage you to talk with your mentor or mentors about the specific time-management issues that are most concerning to you: some new teachers want help managing the amount of time they spend grading, others are concerned with the time needed to create strong lesson plans, and other teachers struggle with finding the time to keep their classrooms organized when there is so much else to do. Like with the instructional suggestions you receive, some time-management recommendations your mentor or mentors recommend will fit with your instructional philosophy, while others may not: it's entirely your prerogative as a teacher to decide what advice you'll follow and what you won't. During my first year of teaching, I was looking for recommendations on responding to student work in effective ways while still doing so quickly enough that the work would be fresh in students' minds when I returned the essays with my comments. Some recommendations I received didn't align with what I felt my students needed, but others, such as remembering to be selective in the feedback I offered students, allowed me to respond to the pieces faster while still providing my students with useful comments.

As the information in this section suggests, mentors can benefit new English teachers in a variety of ways. In the next part of this chapter, we'll look at the mentoring process in action by considering my experiences requesting and acting on advice from my mentorship network as a first-year English teacher.

What Does It Look Like in Action?

Flash back to 2004, my first year of teaching—I'm a seventh-grade English teacher at a public middle school in Brooklyn, NY, and the assistant coach for the school's after-school soccer program. On the whole, my school year's going well: I've been able to integrate a lot of the attributes of the reading and writing workshop curriculum I studied in my teacher-preparation program, I get along well with my students, and I've been pleased with how hard they've been working.

However, I've recently noticed that a number of my students have struggled to understand writing strategies: specifically, how and why published authors use particular tactics such as sensory imagery, prepositional phrases, and strong verbs to maximize the effectiveness of their pieces. I've conducted mini-lessons on key, grade-appropriate writing strategies and shown students published examples. While some students are making great progress, others continue to struggle.

I decide to enlist the help of my mentorship network to help me with this challenge. I have a strong group of mentors: a wonderful official mentor that was assigned to me by the New York City Department of Education, several experienced colleagues that have reached out to me and communicated that they're willing to help, and my former student-teaching supervisor. First, I talk to my colleagues about my experiences up to this point teaching writing strategies to my students, focusing on what I've done, what's worked, what hasn't, and what I want my students to be able to do. They provide a number of ideas based on what's worked for them; I take notes on their insights. That evening, I call my official mentor, who gives me some recommendations and schedules a time to come visit my class and observe what's working and what changes I might make. Before going to bed that night, I send an email to my former student-teaching supervisor who observed me multiple times while a was student teaching as part of my teacher preparation program. The next morning, I wake up to a helpful email from him.

Before school starts the next day, I consider the suggestions I've received. Some are practices I'm already employing, while a few aren't aligned with my educational philosophy; however, there's one idea in the recommendations that really stands out to me: connecting writing strategies to students' out-of-school interests. I'm immediately excited by this, but still not totally sure of how I'm going to put it into action. I ask one of my mentor colleagues for any follow-up tips she has; she tells me to listen to the students when they talk about their interests and think of ways to help them make connections.

Later that day at soccer practice, I hear some of my students thoughtfully analyzing the lyrics of some popular Jay-Z songs. They're not talking about specific writing strategies in their analyses, but it's clear from how carefully they're considering the songs that they could be. I decide that I'm going to spend the weekend thinking about ways to connect my students' awareness of Jay-Z lyrics to our study of writing strategies. I read about this idea online, looking up research and practitioner-oriented articles on connecting academic content to students' home lives and out-of-school interests, ask my mentors some follow-up questions, and put together a plan.

The following Monday, I talk with my students about how the writing strategies we've been discussing are represented in a number of current song lyrics and give them an assignment that asks them to identify song lyrics of their choice (as long they're school-appropriate) and give a presentation to the class that discusses which of our focal writing strategies are important to the effectiveness of those song lyrics. The project turns out extremely well—students are engaged and learn a great deal, and I continue to use versions of that assignment throughout my career as an educator. Once the students' have completed their works, I send emails to all of my mentors thanking them; if not for their advice, this project would never have happened.

Key Tips

In this section, we'll examine two recommendations for maximizing the effectiveness of working with mentors: 1) communicate your needs clearly and 2) consider information carefully before acting on it. These recommendations can help you receive relevant advice from your mentors and ensure that you employ the suggestions that will help you reach your instructional goals. Let's consider both of these recommendations by reflecting on what each one means and why it can be beneficial.

1. Communicate your needs clearly.

For an excellent mentor-mentee relationship to exist, there needs to be more than a helpful and responsive mentor: there also needs to be a mentee who clearly expresses what he or she needs and is interested in learning. When communicating with your mentor, make sure you express exactly what questions you want him or her to answer and what information you want him or her to provide. While having a general conversation with a mentor about your teaching experiences can be a good way to establish a relationship, I advise only doing that as you get to know each other. After that, approach each conversation with a clear focus and state that focus at the beginning of the meeting, such as "I'm trying to figure out how to get more students to participate in our class discussions of *The Catcher in the Rye*" or "What are some tactics you use to engage students at the beginning of class?" Without concrete questions such as these, it's difficult for mentors to provide their mentees with useful insights. Some mentors will still provide you with suggestions even if you don't ask specific questions, but these suggestions may not be related to topics you're interested in or need help with. To make meetings with mentors as effective as possible, be clear about what the areas in which you'd like extra support and guidance.

2. Consider information carefully before acting on it.

Although your mentors are experienced teachers with a great deal of insights, it's important to remember it's up to you to determine whether or not to integrate a mentor's suggestion into your instruction. Most likely, you'll receive some suggestions from your mentors that you immediately think are great ideas, some that you think could work with some adaptations, and some that you don't think will work particularly well for you—and that's all perfectly okay. In the description earlier in this chapter of how I incorporated my students' interests into my writing instruction, I mentioned that I didn't act on every suggestion I received from my mentorship network. I reflected on each one, asking myself, "Is the something that fits with who I am as a teacher?" and "Do I think it would work with my students?" If I couldn't answer "yes" to both questions, I didn't incorporate that practice.

Thinking carefully about each recommendation you receive from a mentor is important to your development as a teacher: throughout your teaching career, you'll receive many suggestions, ideas, and resources; it will always be up to you to decide if you'd like to incorporate that information into your instruction. You can certainly add a new resource or idea to your teaching repertoire, but be sure you're not doing so just because it's a new idea or someone told you to; make your instructional choices based on how they align with the teaching practices you feel are effective and if you feel they'll help your students learn.

Final Thoughts on Working Effectively with Mentors

- ◆ A key component of getting your career as an English teacher off to a strong start is working effectively with a mentor or network of mentors that supports and guides you (Portner, 2008).
- ◆ Three kinds of mentors you might encounter as a new teacher are assigned mentors, naturally developing mentors, and online mentoring communities.
  - ◆ Assigned mentors are experienced teachers that schools or districts match with new ones; they are responsible for introducing their mentees to the school culture and serving as a resource for questions and concerns the mentees have.
  - ◆ Naturally developing mentoring relationships develop over time as you get to know other teachers in your school and notice attributes they have that you'd like to emulate.
  - ◆ Online mentoring communities are groups of teachers who connect using technological resources such as message boards and Twitter chats to communicate, ask questions, and support each other.
- ◆ All of these mentor types can form the basis of one's Professional Learning Network (PLN), "a vibrant, ever-changing group of connections to which teachers go to both share and learn" (Crowley, 2014).
- ◆ I've identified three especially significant ways mentoring can improve the experiences and effectiveness of new teachers:

mentors can help new teachers feel part of a community, mentors can provide instructional ideas, mentors can offer guidance with managing time.

- ◆ Mentors can help new teachers feel part of a community by giving them opportunities to share their successes and challenges with supportive colleagues and reducing feelings of isolation that can accompany one's first year of teaching.
- ◆ Mentors can provide new teachers with instructional ideas by giving them suggestions and resources that can be used to achieve specific instructional goals.
- ◆ Mentors can offer guidance with managing time by providing their mentees with recommendations for ways to handle time-management challenges particularly relevant to mentees' individual experiences.

◆ To maximize the effectiveness of working with your mentors, I recommend following these two suggestions, which can help you receive relevant advice from your mentors and ensure that you employ the suggestions that will help you reach your instructional goals:

- ◆ Communicate your needs clearly.
- ◆ Consider information carefully before acting on it.

11

Make Time for Self-Care

In this chapter, we'll address an aspect of life as a new teacher that can be easily neglected, but is crucial to work-life balance: making time for self-care. First, we'll explore some ways to increase your level of self-care during your first year of teaching. After that, we'll consider why making time to take care of yourself is so important to being a successful first-year teacher. Then, I'll share an example of how I focused on self-care during my first year of teaching; finally, we'll look together at some key recommendations to consider as you make time for self-care in your first year as a teacher.

What Is It?

Self-care can take many forms—for the purposes of this chapter, we'll view it as any activity that maximizes your physical and/or mental health and can contribute to your effectiveness as a teacher. In this section, we'll take a look at some self-care activities that can help sustain your health and therefore contribute to a happy and successful first year of teaching: meditation, exercise, and work-free socializing time. Let's explore some ways to integrate these activities into your everyday routine.

Meditation

If you've never meditated before, your first year of teaching is the ideal time to get started; if you have meditated, this year is a great to time build on the benefits you've likely already experienced. While there are many varieties of meditation (a Google search for "Types of Meditation" can provide you with numerous detailed descriptions of different meditation styles and their distinguishing features), this section focuses on general meditative practices designed to promote mindfulness and relieve stress. To integrate these meditative practices into your daily routine as a new English teacher, I recommend taking some time before school each day (or as many days as possible) to sit somewhere quiet, breathe deeply, and clear your mind. A great benefit of this practice that I've experienced is starting each day with a calm, clear, and focused mentality. When I meditate before a school day starts, I find that I focus far less on stressors from the previous day, such as which students misbehaved or parts of the preceding day's lesson that didn't go as well as I wanted. Meditating before I teach helps me focus on the day, students, and instruction at hand.

Exercise

I highly recommend incorporating a regular exercise program into the daily routine of your first year of teaching. It may sound counterintuitive to recommend extra physical activity during a year when you'll be getting used a to job that will regularly leave you feeling exhausted, but exercising regularly can enhance your mood, increase your energy level, and further promote the mental clarity that meditation can help achieve. During my first year of teaching, I ran frequently, training for and completing the Philadelphia and Boston marathons that year. There's no one form of exercise that I recommend over others: any fitness activity can boost your mood, energy, and mental clarity. Whether you exercise in through one activity or in a variety of ways, I recommend trying to find a regular workout time and exercising during that time as much as possible. I like to run after classes on school days; my runs form excellent bookends with my morning meditation and allow me a way to decompress after a busy day of teaching, but others might prefer exercising before school or simply find that time frame more feasible. No matter what kind of exercise you prefer to do or when you like to do it, I strongly encourage you to work out as regularly as you can. Your first year of teaching will be challenging—the benefits of exercise can give you the boost you need to navigate some of those challenges.

Work-Free Socializing Time

Another way to take care of yourself during your first year of teaching is to make sure that you spend time talking about topics other than your job. As a first-year teacher, it's so easy to discuss work all the time: your family and friends will likely ask you teaching-focused questions when they see you, inquiring about your school, the students, the texts you're teaching, and other related topics because they want to support you at this important stage of your career. Plus, the amount of work we take home as teachers often results in us thinking about our jobs during much of the time we're not at school. At the beginning of my first year of teaching, I spent so much thinking about school and doing school-related work at home that I felt like I never left work! To address this, I identified times during which I would give myself a brain-break from my work as a teacher. For example, when I met up with friends to watch my undergraduate alma mater's college football team, I told my friends that those were times I'd designated as a mental reprieve from work and was open to talking about any topic besides teaching. I strongly encourage you to schedule time during your first year of teaching when you're not going to talk about or think about teaching: this break can help you be more focused when you return your attention to teaching-oriented tasks.

Why Does It Matter?

Now that we've looked at examples of self-care activities, let's consider some reasons why making time to self-care is important to the experience of a first-year English teacher: 1) meeting your own needs helps you meet your students' needs, 2) taking care of yourself helps you navigate challenging situations, and 3) making time for self-care increases your longevity as a teacher. In this section, we'll explore each of these benefits individually.

Meeting Your Own Needs Helps You Meet Your Students' Needs

As a teacher, you'll be called upon to meet your students' needs in a variety of ways (Brookfield, 2015); in addition to helping them academically, there may be times when you'll support your students through personal struggles, family issues, college and career-related decisions, and even physical ailments. I've found it much easier to provide my students with a high level of support when I feel rested, energetic, and focused. On days when I've felt overworked and stressed, it's been much harder for me to provide a caring and supportive presence. Our students want us to balance our classroom authority with a caring presence that communicates we're their allies (Brookfield, 2015); taking care of ourselves through meditation, exercise, and downtime can provide us with the patience and reflectiveness needed to maintain that presence.

Taking Care of Yourself Helps You Navigate Challenging Situations

During your first year of teaching, you're likely to encounter a number of difficult scenarios, such as classroom management issues, the stress of standardized tests, and tough conversations with parents (Mader, 2016). Handling these challenging situations effectively isn't easy and will require a great deal of patience and understanding—when I deal with a difficult teaching-related scenario, I take a deep breath and try to consider all of the circumstances surrounding the event so that I can understand it from as many perspectives as possible. To reach this level of calmness and awareness, I must be in a good place myself: if I'm tired, stressed, or upset, it's much harder for me to navigate these circumstances. By taking care of yourself, you'll increase your ability to effectively deal with the difficult situations you're likely to face as a first-year teacher. If you feel yourself getting frustrated and overwhelmed, reflect on if you're taking enough time for your own needs and look for ways to integrate more self-care into your routine: your students will ultimately thank you for it.

Making Time for Self-Care Increases Your Longevity as a Teacher
While it's long been understood that many new teachers leave the profession (Ingersoll, 2003), more recent research on this topic has revealed that teacher burnout is a significant factor in these decisions to leave (Richards, 2012). Fortunately, the self-care tactics described in this chapter will help you guard against feeling burned out: by taking the time to work out, meditate, and relax with non-school-related conversation, you'll prioritize your mental and physical health and maintain a sense of work-life balance. I believe that having a sense of balance between teaching and self-care is integral to a teacher's longevity. We teachers we have a responsibility to work hard at our jobs and provide our students with the highest quality of instruction, but we also need to take care of ourselves so that we can enjoy full, balanced lives; maintaining that sense of balance will help us be happy, effective teachers for many years.

As the descriptions in this section explain, taking care of yourself will optimize your abilities to do your job as a teacher as effectively as possible. While one's first impulse might be to be a better teacher by throwing her or himself into work, I urge you to balance that hard work with important self-care measures. In the next section, we'll look at a description of a way I worked to maintain work-life balance in a stressful scenario during my first year of teaching and the positive outcome that resulted.

What Does It Look Like in Action?

"Tomorrow's the big day," I say to myself as I leave school on a Thursday afternoon. It's about a month into my first year of teaching and I'm being observed for the first time tomorrow. I've had this day on my calendar for two weeks, starting when my principal told me that she'd scheduled me for an observation: she's coming to see me teach a lesson on sensory imagery to an intelligent (but sometimes rambunctious) class of seventh graders.

I walk down Flatbush Avenue—a busy Brooklyn thoroughfare—to the subway station and with a coworker and fellow first-year teacher. "Are you going to spend all night thinking about the lesson so that you can make everything perfect?" she asks. "That's what I'm going to do when I get observed."

"I planned the lesson earlier this week, so I'm actually going to go for a run when I get home," I respond. "I'll look over the lesson again before dinner and then do some grading after dinner."

"Wow," she responds. "That's great. I think I'd be more nervous and would stay up late planning."

"I'm nervous," I smile, "but I know I have everything set for the lesson—I'm really happy with my plan and my students are prepared to do the activities, so I'm working on making sure I keep balance in my schedule. I'm still keeping my afternoon running and morning meditation schedule; I think taking time for myself will help me teach the lesson better than if I let myself get worried about it."

(It's important to note that I had found it relatively easy to keep my schedule balanced because I was planned and prepared for the observation lesson. Staying on top of one's work makes it easier to partake in self-care activities.)

After an afternoon run, an evening lesson-planning and grading session, and a morning meditation time, I arrive at school ready to go. The class goes extremely well, I'm relaxed, my lesson is engaging, the students convey their intelligence and preparation through insightful responses in our class discussion and strong work in the application components of the instructional period. There are a couple of times when student behavior issues begin to emerge, but I'm able to quickly and calmly take care of these potential problems before anything of substance comes from them. I feel that my self-care routine—in combination with my thorough preparation for this lesson—helped the observation go so well. Running and meditating helped me approach the day with a calm, confident mentality, allowing me to perform to the best of my abilities and not be overwhelmed by nerves.

The next week I have a post-observation conference with my principal, and it turns out she agrees with me. She commends me on the students' interest levels, my interactive instructional activities, and the calm confidence I exuded during the lesson, noting that most people are very nervous when they're first observed, but she didn't notice that from me. I smile, thankful for my self-care routine and its importance to me delivering a successful lesson in a high-pressure situation.

Key Tips

In this section, we'll look at two key recommendations that can help you integrate the self-care practices described in this chapter as effectively as possible: 1) don't wait to be overworked before looking for balance and 2) schedule your self-care time. Each of these suggestions can help you navigate the challenges of being a first-year teaching with a balanced and proactive routine. Let's consider what each one of these tips means and why it can be beneficial.

1. Don't wait to be overworked before looking for balance.

To make your self-care routine as effective as possible, I strongly encourage you to begin your routine before you start feeling overworked. While it may feel tempting to say, "I'll take more time for myself once I notice my work-life balance being a problem," that approach is far less likely to be effective: it's easy to rationalize to yourself that you're not overworking yourself even when you actually are. Plus, it can be much harder to get into a routine once the school year has started and you've grown accustomed to certain patterns and behaviors. Proactively incorporating self-care into your routine will not only reduce your stress level, but can prevent some stress from ever occurring at all. During my first year of teaching, I started my routine of running, meditating, and scheduling downtime before the school year even started, which reduced my baseline stress level going into the school year. While there's no way for me to know how much more stressed I might have been during that year if I didn't take part in a number of self-care activities, the calmness and composure I was able to maintain throughout the school year suggested that my self-care routine optimized my effectiveness. Had I waited until I felt stressed and overwhelmed to begin these activities, I doubt I would you have experienced the same results.

2. Schedule your self-care time.

To maximize the likelihood that you participate in self-care actions like the ones described in this chapter, I recommend keeping a regular schedule of those activities. Depending on your other commitments, you might schedule routines like exercise and meditation for regular times, or vary them daily based on other events taking place those days; what's most important is that you plan when you'll participate in these activities—making a plan will enhance the likelihood that they occur. I like exercising in the afternoon and meditating in the morning, but others might prefer switching the times of these activities, doing both in the afternoon, doing both in the morning, or alternating the activities at a particular time: I worked with a teacher who worked out three weekday mornings a week and meditated the other two. You might try experimenting with some different times and activities and seeing what works best for you; once you find a good fit, you can then make that routine your regular schedule. I've found that keeping myself to a regular schedule is the best way to ensure I'm consistently incorporating self-care into my life; even if I'm doing activities that I enjoy, it can be difficult for me to regularly take part in them if I don't have a specific time designated for them to take place. A self-care schedule can help you integrate these activities into your first year of teaching.

Final Thoughts on Making Time for Self-Care

- ◆ In this context, self-care is any activity that maximizes your physical and/or mental health and can contribute to your effectiveness as a teacher.
- ◆ Three self-care activities that can help sustain your health and contribute to a happy and successful first year of teaching are meditation, exercise, and "no work" socializing time.
  - ◆ Meditation is a great way to help you start each day with a calm, clear, and focused mentality.
  - ◆ Exercise can enhance your mood, increase your energy level, and further promote the mental clarity that meditation can help achieve.
  - ◆ Socializing without talking about work gives you a brain-break that can help you be more focused when you return your attention to teaching-oriented tasks.
- ◆ I've identified three reasons why making time to self-care is important to the experience of a first-year English teacher: meeting your own needs helps you meet your students' needs, taking care of yourself helps you navigate challenging situations, and making time for self-care increases your longevity as a teacher.
  - ◆ Meeting your own needs through self-care activities such as meditation, exercise, and downtime can provide you with the patience and reflectiveness needed to support your students.
  - ◆ By taking care of yourself, you'll increase your ability to effectively deal with the difficult situations (such as classroom management issues, the stress of standardized tests, and tough conversations with parents) you're likely to face as a first-year teacher.
  - ◆ Taking time for self-care increases longevity by reducing the likelihood that you'll feel burned out by teaching; research reveals many teachers who leave the profession due so do to feeling burned out (Richards, 2012).
- ◆ When integrating the self-care practices described in this chapter, keep these recommendations in mind; they can help you navigate the challenges of being a first-year teaching with a balanced and proactive routine:
  - ◆ Don't wait to be overworked before looking for balance.
  - ◆ Schedule your self-care time.

Section 4

Resources

12

Key Takeaway Ideas

Now that you've read the first eleven chapters of this book, you've developed understandings of important instructional, assessment, and work-life balance strategies that will help you achieve success during your first year as an English teacher. In this final chapter, I'll share four key ideas for you to consider when putting the ideas in this book into action:

- ◆ Instructional practices and procedures impact student learning and behavior
- ◆ A reflective approach to instruction leads to thoughtful, high-quality decisions
- ◆ Clear and focused feedback is crucial to student success and teacher sanity
- ◆ Balance is essential to success

These statements synthesize important information described in *The First-Year English Teacher's Guidebook*, providing some key takeaway ideas for you to reflect on throughout your first year of teaching English. If you decide during the school year that you want a brief overview of major insights from this book, I recommend rereading this chapter for key highlights and points of information. Then, if you feel you want more detail about a specific instructional practice or idea referred to in a section of this chapter, you can reexamine the chapter in the book specifically dedicated to that concept. (For example, if you want additional reminders about conducting writing conferences, you can revisit Chapter Seven.) Now, let's consider each of these insights in detail.

Instructional Practices and Procedures Impact Student Learning and Behavior

A key differentiating factor between an effective and ineffective class is the kind of instructional practices and procedures used (Wong & Wong, 2009). An English class with effective instructional practices and procedures can feel like it runs on its own: students know what to do, where to go, and what materials to use at specifically designated times. The efficiency of a well-organized class enhances both the quality of students' behavior and their learning: an English class that is focused on specific learning outcomes and contains minimal disruptions will maximize the material students learn. Many of the insights in this book will help you incorporate practices and procedures that optimize student behavior and learning: Chapter One shares strategies for establishing focal questions and well-structured agendas for each class period that will keep students focused and engaged, Chapter Three discusses how clear organization, a strong sense of pace, and a thorough lesson plan are important to facilitating student learning and encouraging effective behavior, and Chapter Eight describes how the use of exit questions can provide a sense of closure to a class period while also helping students reflect on the material they've learned that day. As you reflect on the instructional practices and classroom procedures you use in your classes, remember that instruction and classroom management are related concepts: by planning engaging, well-structured lessons with smooth transitions, you'll keep your students on-tasks while optimizing their learning.

A Reflective Approach to Instruction Leads to Thoughtful, High-Quality Decisions

Throughout your career as a teacher, you'll encounter countless instructional strategies that others will recommend: some of these will enhance your teaching, while others won't. Some ideas will be research-based and classroom-tested; others might be gimmicky and not based on quality evidence. To make decisions about the ideas and strategies you'll integrate into your instruction, I suggest taking a reflective approach to the recommendations you encounter. To do this, ask yourself questions about whether or not the strategies will have positive impacts on your instruction. Questions like "How will this strategy improve my instruction?" "Will it help me teach my students more effectively?" and "Will it enhance my students' abilities to learn important material?" will help you carefully consider the effectiveness of the instructional recommendations you're considering. Chapter Two of this book discusses ideas for integrating students' out-of-school lives into your English instruction and Chapter Four outlines an approach for ensuring that you're using technology in a way that enhances student learning. No matter the specific instructional idea you're considering, take the time to reflect on whether or not it will enhance your teaching (and if so, how); this framework will help you make strong decisions for yourself and your students.

Clear and Focused Feedback Is Crucial to Student Success and Teacher Sanity

As an English teacher, you're going to spend a lot of time responding to student writing: your students will write pieces in a number of genres, such as narrative, argument, informational, and literary analysis. When you respond to and evaluate student work, I strongly recommend keeping your comments and reactions as clear and focused as possible. Some English teachers look at a piece of student writing and want to fix it in every way possible; while this approach may be guided by good intentions, it isn't useful for the students or the teacher. When you comment on a student's writing—whether in a one-on-one conference or a written response—your feedback will be most useful if you make specific suggestions for improvement that are relevant to what your students' understand and provide them with concrete praise.

It's important that your suggestions are specific so that students know exactly what they can do to make their work better. Similarly, your feedback should be related to what students know and are able to do so that they can make the changes you recommend—there's no point in making recommendations that are beyond students' abilities. Concrete and specific responses will not only give your students clear understandings of what they should work and what they're already doing well, but also will allow you to use your grading time more effectively and efficiently: giving your students focused and relevant feedback takes less time than correcting every error. Chapter Five of this book describes tactics for creating assignment-specific rubrics that reflect your instruction, Chapter Six provides insights for composing concrete and useful written responses to student work, and Chapter Seven discusses strategies for holding individual writing conferences with students that focus on the specific attributes of their works. When providing students with feedback on their pieces, use these ideas to help you provide concrete, useful, and relevant information they can use to enhance their writing (while also reducing the likelihood that you'll be up all night long grading!).

Balance Is Essential to Success

The final idea I'd like you to consider is that a sense of balance is essential to your success as an English teacher during your first year and throughout the rest of your career. As Chapters Nine through Eleven in this book describe, work-life balance can take many forms. The active communication strategies illustrated in Chapter Nine promote a sense of balance by facilitating the flow of your instruction, forming connections with that can result in them supporting you at home, and making your students responsible for using the resources you've provided. The ideas on working with mentors discussed in Chapter Ten can facilitate balance in your life by giving you the tools you need to ask those in your mentorship networks for advice and the strategies to make informed decisions about whether you should follow that advice. Finally, the suggestions in Chapter Eleven will help you incorporate a self-care routine into your daily schedule; such a routine can maximize your effectiveness as a teacher and help extend your career by reducing the likelihood that you'll overwhelmed and burned out.

A Final Thought

As you put this book into action and integrate its ideas into your work as a teacher, I encourage you to think of it as a map to a successful first year of teaching English. The instructional ideas discussed in Section One, the assessment tactics presented in Section Two, and work-life balance recommendations described in Section Three are designed to work together to provide you with a thorough repertoire of skills and strategies you can use to make your first year of teaching English an enjoyable and productive experience for you and your students. I want to close by congratulating you on choosing such an important career; there are times when it will be difficult, but there are also times when you will experience the successes that make this work so rewarding. Your work with your students will make a huge impact on their lives. Use this book as a guide to help you do so, and please don't hesitate to reach out to me with any questions. I'm thrilled that you're joining me in this fantastic profession.

References

Bratcher, S., & Ryan, L. (2004). *Evaluating children's writing* (2nd ed.). Mahwah, NJ: Lawrence Earlbaum Associates.

Brookfield, S. D. (2015). *The skillful teacher: On technique, trust, and responsiveness in the classroom* (3rd ed.). San Francisco, CA: Jossey-Bass.

Campbell, B. (2009). To-with-by: A three-tiered model for differentiated instruction. *The NERA Journal, 44*(2), 7–10.

Common Core State Standards Initiative. (2010). *Common core state standards for English language arts.* Retrieved from www.corestandards.org.

Cormier, R. (1974). *The chocolate war.* New York, NY: Bantam Doubleday Dell.

Crowley, R. (2014). Three steps for building a professional learning network. *Education Week Teacher.* Retrieved from www.edweek.org/tm/articles/2014/12/31/3-steps-for-building-a-professional-learning.html

Culham, R. (2003). *6 + 1 traits of writing.* New York, NY: Scholastic.

Cushman, K. (2005). *Fires in the bathroom: Advice for teachers from high school students.* New York, NY: The New Press.

Duncan-Andrade, J., & Morrell, E. (2005). Turn up that radio, teacher: Popular cultural pedagogy in new century urban schools. *Journal of School Leadership, 15*(3), 284–304.

Ferris, D. (2007). Preparing teachers to respond to student writing. *Journal of Second Language Writing, 16,* 165–193.

Fisher, D., & Frey, N. (2003). Writing instructional for struggling adolescent readers: A gradual release model. *Journal of Adolescent and Adult Literacy, 46*(5), 396–407.

Fitzgerald, F. S. (1925). *The great Gatsby.* New York, NY: Charles Scribner's Sons.

Fleischman, P. (1997). *Seedfolks.* New York, NY: HarperCollins.

Fletcher, R., & Portalupi, J. (2001). *Writing workshop: The essential guide.* Portsmouth, NH: Heinemann.

Fry, S. W. (2007). First-year teachers and induction support: Ups, downs, and in-betweens. *The Qualitative Report, 12*(2), 216–237.

Goodwin, B. (2012). Research says new teachers face three common challenges. *Educational Leadership, 69*(8), 84–85.

Grisham, D. L., & Wolsey, T. D. (2006). Recentering the middle school classroom as a vibrant learning community: Students, literacy, and technology intersect. *Journal of Adolescent & Adult Literacy, 49*(8), 648–660.

Holaday, L. (1997). Writing students need coaches, not judges. In S. Tchudi (Ed.), *Alternatives to grading student writing* (p. 35). Urbana, IL: NCTE.

Ingersoll, R. (2003). *Is there really a teacher shortage?* Philadelphia, PA: University of Pennsylvania, Consortium for Policy Research in Education.

Jago, C. (2005). *Papers, papers, papers: An English teacher's survival guide.* Portsmouth, NH: Heinemann.

Kent, A. M., Green, A. M., & Feldman, P. (2012). Fostering the success of new teachers: Developing lead teachers in a statewide teacher mentoring program. *Current Issues in Education, 15*(3), 1–15.

Klass, D. (1994). *California blue.* New York, NY: Scholastic.

Ladson-Billings, G. (1995). But that's just good teaching! The case for culturally-relevant pedagogy. *Theory into Practice, 34*(3), 159–165.

Mader, J. (2016). The first year of teaching can feel like a fraternity hazing. *The Atlantic.* Retrieved from www.theatlantic.com/education/archive/2016/04/first-year-teaching/477990/

Pasternak, D. L. (2007). Is technology used as practice? A survey analysis of preservice English teachers' perceptions and classroom practices. *Contemporary Issues in Technology and Teacher Education, 7*(3), 140–157.

Pope, C., & Golub, J. (2000). Preparing tomorrow's English language arts teachers today: Principles and practices for infusing technology. *Contemporary Issues in Technology and Teacher Education, 1,* 89–97.

Portner, H. (2008). *Mentoring new teachers* (3rd ed.). Thousand Oaks, CA: Corwin Press.

Richards, J. (2012). Teacher stress and coping strategies: A national snapshot. *Educational Forum, 76,* 299–316.

Ruday, S. (2016). *The argument writing toolkit.* New York, NY: Routledge.

Shea, M. (2015). Differentiating writing instruction: Meeting the diverse needs of authors in a classroom. *Journal of Inquiry and Action in Education, 6*(2), 80–118.

Sutcher, L., Darling-Hammond, L., & Carver-Thomas, D. (2016). *A coming crisis in teaching? Teacher supply, demand, and shortages in the U.S.* Palo Alto, CA: Learning Policy Institute.

Wolsey, T. D., & Grisham, P. D. L. (2012). *Transforming writing instruction in the digital age: Techniques for grades 5–12.* New York, NY: Guilford Press.

Wong, H. K., & Wong, R. T. (2009). *The first days of school: How to be an effective teacher* (4th ed.). Mountain View, CA: Harry K. Wong Publications.

Woolf, V. ([1925] 2005). *Mrs. Dalloway.* New York, NY: Harcourt Brace and Company.

Young, C. A., & Bush, J. (2004). Teaching the English language arts with technology: A critical approach and pedagogical framework. *Contemporary Issues in Technology and Teacher Education, 4*(1), 1–22.

Forms, Templates, and Graphic Organizers

Figure 1.6 Big Question Planning Template

Instructional Focus	Question(s) Related to Instructional Focus	Examples
Fundamental components		How do writers acknowledge alternate and opposing claims in their argument essays?
Significance and application		Why is this an important aspect of strong argument essays? How can we apply this strategy to our own essays?

Figure 1.7 "To, With, and By" Agenda Planning Template

Agenda Section	Activity	Example Activity
To		Mini-lesson on activity acknowledging alternate opposing claims
With		Group discussion of identifying and analyzing acknowledgments of alternate and opposing claims
By		Students work on acknowledging alternate and opposing claims in their own works

Figure 2.4 Graphic Organizer for Vocative Social Media Analysis

Social Media Post	Explanation of How It Does or Does Not Use a Screenname as a Vocative

Figure 2.5 Out-of-School Connection Content Planning Guide

Academic Topic on Which You're Focusing	Related Out-of-School Content	Why You Believe the Topic and Content Relate

Figure 3.3 Graphic Organizer for Power Analysis Activity

Quotation from Text	What You Can Infer about Power in the Scenario

Figure 4.1 Graphic Organizer for Argument Essay Image Analysis

Topic	Your Response
Your essay's argument	
Description of an image related to your essay's topic that does not support your argument	
Why this image does not support your essay's argument	
Description of an image related to your essay's topic that supports your argument	
Why this image supports your essay's argument	

Figure 4.2 Graphic Organizer for Evaluating Technology Use

Component	Your Response
The specific way technology will be used	
Key benefits associated with using technology in this way	
How these benefits can enhance student learning	

Figure 5.2 Assignment-Specific Rubric for an Argument Essay

Component	Evaluation Criteria	Possible Points	Your Score
Introducing claims	◆ Does the introductory paragraph effectively communicate to readers the issue the rest of the piece will be describing? ◆ Does the author clearly communicate his or her position on this issue?	4	
Acknowledging alternate or opposing claims	◆ Does the piece clearly incorporate an alternate or opposing view that differs from the author's claim? ◆ Does the piece include information that refutes this alternate or opposing claim?	4	
Organizing reasons and evidence logically	◆ Are the essay's paragraphs clearly divided into separate ideas? ◆ Are the paragraphs sequenced in a logical way, such as beginning with an introduction, moving to paragraphs that support the piece's claim, transitioning to discussions of alternate or opposing claims, and then finishing with a concluding section?	4	
Creating an effective concluding section	◆ Does the conclusion emphasize the significance of the cause for which the essay is arguing? ◆ Does the conclusion leave readers with a final thought about the piece's claim?	4	

Component	Evaluation Criteria	Possible Points	Your Score
Supporting details	◆ Are the ideas and insights in the essay supported by relevant details that clearly relate to the points they are supporting?	4	
Strong mechanics	◆ Does the piece demonstrate an understanding of proper punctuation? ◆ Are sentences clear and representative of complete thoughts? ◆ Is capitalization used at appropriate times?	4	

This rubric is adapted from my book *The Argument Writing Toolkit* (Ruday, 2016).

Figure 5.3 Example of Criteria-Referenced Rubric

Component	Evaluation Criteria	Possible Points	Your Score
Ideas	◆ Is the piece's central idea clear? ◆ Is the idea supported with relevant details?	4	
Voice	◆ Is there a clear sense of voice to the piece? ◆ Is it clear what the author wants the reader to feel?	4	
Organization	◆ Is the piece structured in a logical way? ◆ Are the sections of the piece organized based on common characteristics? ◆ Do these sections convey meaning with their order?	4	
Word choice	◆ Does the piece include a variety of vocabulary? ◆ Does the piece use specific language that aligns with the intended meaning?	4	
Sentence fluency	◆ Does the piece include a range of sentence constructions (such as simple, compound, and complex sentences)? ◆ Are these sentence constructions used in ways that align with the information the author is attempting to convey?	4	
Conventions	◆ Does the author demonstrate a mastery of capitalization, punctuation, and spelling?	4	

Figure 5.4 Event-Focused Poetry Rubric

Component	Evaluation Criteria	Possible Points	Your Score
Focus	◆ Does the poem clearly focus on a singular event in the speaker's life?	4	
Detail	◆ Is the event described in detail? ◆ Do the descriptive details used make it easy for readers to understand the key components of the event?	4	
Concrete language	◆ Does the poem use concrete language, such as specific nouns and strong verbs? ◆ Is the concrete language relevant to the poem and used in a way that contributes to readers' understandings of it?	4	
Stanzas	◆ Does the poem contain at least two stanzas? ◆ Are the stanzas organized purposefully in ways that correspond with distinct aspects of the poem?	4	
Message	◆ Does the poem deliver a clear message about why the event is significant to the speaker's life?	4	

Figure 5.5 Washington, DC, Monument Essay Rubric

Component	Evaluation Criteria	Possible Points	Your Score
Organization	◆ Does each one of the essay's paragraphs have a central focus? ◆ Do the paragraphs logically flow from one to the next?	4	
History	◆ Does the essay provide a detailed description of the monument's history, paying special attention to important people, events, and dates?	4	
Features	◆ Does the essay describe the monument's key features in detail, indicating that the author has an excellent understanding of these attributes?	4	
Significance	◆ Does the essay provide a detailed discussion of the monument's historical and cultural significance, including information about what the message the monument sends?	4	
Introduction	◆ Does the essay's introduction grab the reader's attention and clearly convey what the essay is about?	4	
Conclusion	◆ Does the conclusion leave readers with a final thought or message about the monument? ◆ Does it go beyond summarizing the essay's content?	4	
Sources	◆ Does the essay cite current, unbiased, and reputable sources for its information when applicable and appropriate?	4	

Component	Evaluation Criteria	Possible Points	Your Score
Mechanics	◆ Does the piece demonstrate an understanding of proper punctuation (especially when integrating quotations and outside sources into the essay)? ◆ Are sentences clear and representative of complete thoughts?	4	

Figure 7.1 Writing Conference Procedures

Order	Action
Step one	Ask the student to summarize the piece she or he is writing.
Step two	Ask the student to explain what she or he has done so far and what she or he plans to do.
Step three	Have the student read her or his piece out loud. While the student does this, make notes about specific strengths of the piece and ways the piece could be even stronger.
Step four	Share with the student a specific strength of the piece, citing specific evidence.
Step five	Make one suggestion for enhancing the piece by either introducing a new writing strategy or revisiting one you've previously taught. Provide the student with concrete recommendations for how this strategy could be integrated into her or his work.

Figure 7.4 Writing Conference Documentation Form

Student name and date	
Current piece	
Notes about piece	
What I most liked	
What I taught and why	

Figure 7.5 Guidelines for Students Who Need Help During Independent Writing

---

What to do if you need help during independent writing

◆ First, try a reference book! Dictionaries, thesauruses, and style guides are located on the "Reference" shelf of the classroom library.

◆ If that doesn't work, ask someone at your table (if you feel it's a question a peer can answer).

◆ If you still need help, write your name on the whiteboard under the heading "Needs Help." I will come to you as soon as I can. (You can move on to another section of your piece while you wait.)

Appendix B
A Guide for Book Studies

The First-Year English Teacher's Guidebook is well-suited for groups of new English teachers using the text as a book study as they meet and discuss the successes and challenges they're experiencing as first-year teachers. If you are interested in discussing this text with fellow new English teachers, I recommend using this guide to facilitate your conversations. The guide is divided into three sections: before reading, during reading, and after reading; it contains questions and topics to consider at each of these stages. (The during-reading section is further separated into questions related to the book's sections on instructional, assessment, and work-life balance strategies.) The questions in this guide are designed to help you reflect on key issues in the book and spark conversations with your colleagues about how you can apply the ideas in the book to your instruction.

Before Reading

Before beginning your experience reading and discussing *The First-Year English Teacher's Guidebook*, I recommend activating your prior knowledge of the book's central points by considering these key issues:

- As you begin your first year of teaching, what are you most excited about?
- Which aspect of your first year of teaching makes you feel most nervous?
- How do you want your students to describe your instruction?
- What do you feel makes for effective assessment of student work?
- What does the term "work-life balance" mean to you?

During Reading

After reading Chapters One through Four in Section One: Instructional Strategies, answer the following questions:

- What are some benefits that go along with clearly communicating your instructional goals to your students?
- What are some things teachers should consider when incorporating students' out-of-school lives?

- How are classroom procedures and student behavior related?
- How will you purposefully integrate technology in your instruction?

Once you've read Chapters Five through Eight in Section Two: Assessment Strategies, respond to these questions:

- What are some strengths you believe assignment-specific rubrics possess?
- Why is it important to select one or two piece-specific areas of growth when responding to student writing?
- How do you think writing conferences help differentiate the instruction teachers provide their students?
- What are some ways you feel exit questions can inform instruction?

When you've read Chapters Nine through Eleven in Section Three: Work-Life Balance Strategies, answer these three questions:

- Which of the benefits of active communication discussed in Chapter Nine especially stands out to you?
- Chapter Ten recommends that new teachers communicate their needs clearly to their mentors and carefully consider information mentors share before acting on it. Why are these important aspects of working effectively with mentors?
- What are some self-care activities (such as those described in Chapter Eleven) that you'll incorporate in your routine during your first year of teaching? When will you do them?

After Reading

Now that you've completed *The First-Year English Teacher's Guidebook*, respond to these after-reading questions designed to help you synthesize the book's key ideas.

- What is something you read about in this book that surprised you?
- What do you see as the biggest challenge of being a first-year teacher?
  - How will you use the information in this book to help you address that challenge?
- Based on your reading of this book, what is one recommendation you would give other first-year English teachers?
- Complete this statement: "My first year as an English teacher will be a success because I will . . ."

Appendix C
Recommendations for Mastering ELA Content Knowledge

This resource contains specific suggestions for mastering ELA content knowledge, such as texts, writing strategies, and grammatical concepts I recommend teaching in grades six through twelve. The recommendations in this section are based on the Common Core State Standards as well as my own research, classroom experiences, and conversations with students and teachers. The section is divided by grade level, with separate sections for some frequently studied texts, writing strategies, and grammatical concepts for each grade (for example, the seventh-grade section identifies texts often taught in that grade, suggested writing strategies to teach, and grammatical concepts to introduce).

This appendix is meant to provide a starting point for considering key material addressed in each of the grade levels on which this book focuses. When you're beginning your first year of teaching English, be sure to consult with your school's administration to learn if there is a school curriculum guide that you should also examine so you know if there are certain texts and strategies the school's English teachers typically introduce in particular grades. Also, it's important to note that you'll likely have variation in your students' abilities within grades: you might have an eighth-grade class that features some students that can work at the grade level's standards, others that work below those benchmarks, and others with skills and understandings above the standards. In those situations, you'll want to further differentiate your instruction to meet your students' individual needs and abilities—many of the instructional strategies described in Section Two will help you do this.

Sixth Grade

Frequently Studied Texts

- *A Wrinkle in Time*, Madeleine L'Engle
- *Crash*, Jerry Spinelli
- *Miracle's Boys*, Jacqueline Woodson
- *Under a War-Torn Sky*, L. M. Elliott
- *Holes*, Louis Sachar

Writing Strategies

♦ Introducing claims in argument writing and supporting them with reasons and evidence from credible sources.
♦ Effectively organizing an event sequence in narrative writing.
♦ In informational writing, developing a topic with relevant facts, details, quotations, and definitions.

Grammatical Concepts

♦ Using intensive pronouns.
♦ Distinguishing between different pronoun cases (such as subject, object, and possessive cases).
♦ Using punctuation to separate nonrestrictive (or parenthetical) elements from the rest of a sentence.

Seventh Grade

Frequently Studied Texts

♦ *Roll of Thunder, Hear My Cry*, Mildred Taylor
♦ *The House on Mango Street*, Sandra Cisneros
♦ *Seedfolks*, Paul Fleischman
♦ *The True Confessions of Charlotte Doyle*, Avi
♦ *Out of the Dust*, Karen Hesse

Writing Strategies

♦ Organizing reasons and evidence logically in argument writing.
♦ Developing experiences and events in detail in narrative writing.
♦ Using precise language and domain-specific vocabulary to convey important information about a topic in informational writing.

Grammatical Concepts

♦ Purposefully using simple, compound, complex, and compound-complex sentences.
♦ Recognizing and correcting dangling modifiers.
♦ Distinguishing among connotations of words with similar denotations.

Eighth Grade

Frequently Studied Texts

- *To Kill a Mockingbird*, Harper Lee
- *Of Mice and Men*, John Steinbeck
- *Fallen Angels*, Walter Dean Myers
- *The Giver*, Lois Lowry
- *The Outsiders*, S. E. Hinton

Writing Strategies

- Acknowledging and refuting alternate or opposing claims in argument writing.
- Incorporating characterization tactics in narrative writing.
- Organizing ideas, concepts, and information into broader categories in informational writing.

Grammatical Concepts

- Strategically using the active and passive voices.
- Forming and using verbs in the imperative, indicative, interrogative, conditional, and subjunctive moods.
- Employing punctuation—such as a comma, ellipsis, or dash—to indicate a pause or break.

Ninth Grade

Frequently Studied Texts

- *Fahrenheit 451*, Ray Bradbury
- *A Raisin in the Sun*, Lorraine Hansberry
- *The Book Thief*, Marcus Zusak
- *Romeo and Juliet*, William Shakespeare
- *Black Boy*, Richard Wright

Writing Strategies

- Anticipating the audience's knowledge level and potential concerns in argument writing.
- Incorporating complex techniques such as pacing and multiple plot lines into narrative writing.

- Using formatting, graphics, and multimedia in informational writing to aid the audience's comprehension.

Grammatical Concepts

- Using key phrases (such as prepositional, participial, and absolute phrases) to convey specific meanings and add variety to a text.
- Using key clauses (such as relative and subordinate clauses) to convey specific meanings and add variety to a text.

Tenth Grade

Frequently Studied Texts

- *The Metamorphosis*, Franz Kafka
- *1984*, George Orwell
- *The Joy Luck Club*, Amy Tan
- *A Doll's House*, Henrik Ibsen
- *Wuthering Heights*, Elizabeth Bronte

Writing Strategies

- Establishing clear relationships between claims, counterclaims, reasons, and evidence in argument writing.
- Crafting a conclusion in narrative writing that reflects on the narrative's events, ideas, and resolutions.
- Using appropriate and varied transitions in informational writing to link major sections, create cohesion, and clarify relationships.

Grammatical Concepts

- Using semicolons to link closely related independent clauses and maximize the flow of a sentence.
- Interpreting figures of speech and understanding their roles in a text.

Eleventh Grade

Frequently Studied Texts

- *The Scarlet Letter*, Nathaniel Hawthorne
- *The Great Gatsby*, F. Scott Fitzgerald

- *Their Eyes Were Watching God*, Zora Neale Hurston
- *The Bluest Eye*, Toni Morrison
- *Adventures of Huckleberry Finn*, Mark Twain

Writing Strategies

- Conducting both short and in-depth research designed to answer a question or solve a problem.
- While conducting research, gathering relevant information from multiple reputable sources and integrating that information into the text in a way that maintains the flow of the piece.

Grammatical Concepts

- Varying syntax for effect.
- Analyzing nuanced variations in the meanings of words with similar definitions.

Twelfth Grade

Frequently Studied Texts

- *The Canterbury Tales*, Geoffrey Chaucer
- *Don Quixote*, Miguel de Cervantes
- *Crime and Punishment*, Fyodor Dostoevsky
- *The Autobiography of Malcolm X*, Malcolm X and Alex Haley
- *As I Lay Dying*, William Faulkner

Writing Strategies

- Narrowing and broadening research inquiries when appropriate to best achieve the intended objective.
- Drawing evidence from literary and informational texts to support one's research.

Grammatical Concepts

- Using domain-specific words and phrases to express ideas clearly and align a text with the audience's expectations.
- Incorporating these words and phrases into one's written and verbal communication in ways that convey college and career-readiness.